The Rainbow Wheel

The Rainbow Wheel

♦

Thirteen Spiritual Gifts

Jo Elise Friedman, Ph.D.

iUniverse, Inc.
New York Lincoln Shanghai

The Rainbow Wheel
Thirteen Spiritual Gifts

Copyright © 2007 by Jo Elise Friedman

All rights reserved. No part of this book may be used or reproduced by any means, graphic, electronic, or mechanical, including photocopying, recording, taping or by any information storage retrieval system without the written permission of the publisher except in the case of brief quotations embodied in critical articles and reviews.

iUniverse books may be ordered through booksellers or by contacting:

iUniverse
2021 Pine Lake Road, Suite 100
Lincoln, NE 68512
www.iuniverse.com
1-800-Authors (1-800-288-4677)

Because of the dynamic nature of the Internet, any Web addresses or links contained in this book may have changed since publication and may no longer be valid.

ISBN: 978-0-595-43771-9 (pbk)
ISBN: 978-0-595-88099-7 (ebk)

Printed in the United States of America

The views expressed in this work are solely those of the author and do not necessarily reflect the views of the publisher, and the publisher hereby disclaims any responsibility for them.

Cover Art: ©Francene Hart, www. francenehart.com
Cover and Graphic Design: Dan Feller, www.danfellerdesigns.com

Graphic images from Francene Hart's © "KA" painting appear in some of the illustrations, with permission from the artist.

For Wayne and Dan, who always light the way

CONTENTS

PREFACE — xi

INTRODUCTION — xiii

Part I What Is the Rainbow Wheel?

Chapter 1 Light Journeys — 3

Chapter 2 The Story of the Rainbow Wheel — 11

Chapter 3 The Rainbow Wheel Map for Conscious Soul Evolution — 23

Chapter 4 Identifying Your Spiritual Gift — 43

Part II How Does the Rainbow Wheel Map for Conscious Soul Evolution Work?

Chapter 5 Portal One: Invoking Your Spiritual Gift — 61

Chapter 6 Portal Two: Liberating the Gatekeepers — 81

Chapter 7 Portal Three: Spiraling Breath — 105

Chapter 8 Portal Four: Renewing the Genesis Pattern — 115

Part III What's Next on the Rainbow Wheel Pathway?

Chapter 9 Your Spiritual Ancestry — 127

Chapter 10 Presence — 139

Chapter 11 The Shimmering Rainbow Lights of Creation — 151

GLOSSARY	155
CHAPTER NOTES	159
RESOURCES	167
ACKNOWLEDGMENTS	175
ABOUT THE AUTHOR	177

PREFACE

The story of soul is encircling the earth. This narrative thread is being woven from many stories. It comes from the wisdom of the ancients, along with new insights from current investigations, explorations, and dialogues that are emerging around the world. We are engaged in a quest to *know* about soul. At this amazing time of accelerating global connectivity, we are unfolding our understandings in ways not previously imaginable. Pathways for transformation are becoming visible, and we are collectively evolving consciousness and soul.

The thirteenth-century Persian poet Rumi tells us:

Human beings are like creek water.
When it's muddy, you can't see the riverbed where the jewels
are. Let the water be as it was at the origin spring.[1]

The "jewels" have always, *always*, been there. Now, more of us seem to be immersed in a time of seeking to awaken the deeper self and embrace the jewel of soul. We are inviting ourselves to do the inner work that is necessary so that we might clear the waters and return to the "origin spring."

We are living in a magnificent time in which we have ready access to information from the fields of spirituality, religion, quantum science, psychology, philosophy, and consciousness research. This is a time in which we are discovering new ways of understanding the extraordinary, the cosmos, and soul. Scientists, artists, poets, philosophers, and you and I are gathering our collective wisdom. We are poised to draw upon the insights and understandings arising from this unique weaving. As part of this gathering, we are calling to hear each other's stories of life and learning. We yearn to connect with the knowing of others, and to more clearly see possible pathways for awakening and transforming, both as individuals and as a global community.

Author Christina Baldwin describes us as story creators and storytellers, and also as "storycatchers." She writes, "None of us can judge exactly what is needed: we don't know; we just set out the stories because someday, somebody will need these clues … the story that gets one person through makes a map for getting the next person through. Storycatching is really the art of story releasing, of putting good stories out in the world, holding them high and tossing them onto the wind like a hawk taking flight into freedom."[2]

The Rainbow Wheel is the story and the map that I am tossing onto the wind. My story began one quiet summer evening of my youth when I had an ecstatic experience of the pulsating radiance and beauty of the rainbow wheel of lights, a wheel of spiritual gifts. Shaped by time, life's experiences, direct encounters with the light of Spirit, my studies, and my spiritual mentoring work, I have come to understand that our spiritual gifts are entryways for awakening and for conscious soul evolution. As you come to ***Be*** your spiritual gift, you find your pathway to your divine self. This is truly a celebration of light and life—*a celebration of soul.*

INTRODUCTION

◆

Dream Vision

One quiet summer night as I slept, I felt myself floating out the window into a ray of light, leaving behind my back porch bedroom of my family's Chicago apartment. All was still on our dead-end street, which had been filled just a few hours before with the laughter of my neighborhood friends. Now even the river seemed silent. At age five I knew the sensation of floating, like when rising upward in water from the bottom of a pool, yet this was different. "*I*" had floated out of my body, and as I neared the ray of light the sensation of floating was changing to one of flying, swiftly but silently.

As I flew along, like a soaring golden eagle, I felt as though I was looking out of a window. I could see the deep green earth below and sensed that I was looking at the future. There were many villages throughout the countryside, and brilliant, rainbow-colored lines of light connected everything. They vibrated, and in the silence of the evening I could hear their deep, resonant hum. Peace and love were everywhere.

The ray of light suddenly ended at a shimmering opening, a gateway of brilliant yellow and white light, luminous and pulsating. I came to a stop, suspended in wondering, and as I peered into this gateway I saw whirling, rainbow-colored lights. I looked deeply into the light and seemed to "know" things, as if I were reading many books all at once. There was no end to knowing.

Suddenly, I returned home and was standing in my backyard. I looked up into the ray of glistening light, and as it faded away into the night sky I returned to my bedroom, floating through the ceiling and entering my body through the top of my head. The sounds of life around me resumed, and I could once again hear nighttime in my home.

In the morning as soon as I awoke I ran to the window, and looking out into our yard I saw an impression in the grass from which a sparkling light was emanating. I ran to my mother and took her by the hand, dragging her down the back stairs while excitedly explaining my night travels. When we reached the backyard I stood pointing at the light on the grass and said, "See, see! That's where I was standing when I came back!" In her most patient and loving voice she said, "I'm sorry, sweetie, I just don't see it, but I really believe that *you* see it. *I* just can't see it."

I remember looking up at her, my hands on my hips and my feet firmly planted on the ground, thinking that I couldn't believe that she couldn't see it, but I knew she was being honest with me.

This exhilarating dream vision experience stayed with me, and I often excitedly thought about the luminous gateway of light, the brilliant, whirling rainbow colors, and the vision of earth with lines made of light connecting all. Although I would not begin to interpret this experience for many years, this memory brought joy and a sense of purpose as it accompanied me throughout my youth. It has shaped the path of my life as I have come to know the gifts of this expansive portal of light.

PART I
What Is the Rainbow Wheel?

○ ○

The Rainbow Wheel is a whirling wheel of thirteen spiritual gifts. Its radiant rainbow lights offer you a path for exploring how *your* spiritual gift can provide an entryway for awakening and evolving your soul.

The dawn of joy has arisen
and this is the moment of union, of vision.
—Rumi

1

Light Journeys

Forty-three years after my initial dream vision experience, I stood among the redwood trees in Muir Woods on the California coast on a quest to integrate my learning throughout these years of conscious journeying to the portal of rainbow lights. Standing in awe and in silence among the redwood trees brought new reflections. My meditations revealed interconnections between the many pieces I had seen, felt, and sensed throughout the years. Sitting and lying on the forest floor, I listened deeply. Kneeling inside an enormous tree that had been partially hollowed out by fire many years before, yet was still alive and growing, I again listened deeply.

As I did so, I found myself infused with a sense of grace. The fragrance of the bay leaves, even in late fall, was still overpowering. All of my senses were more alive, more present—just more. Then, in a moment of stillness and silence, a swirl of *knowing*, carried on the timeless fragrance and beauty of the trees, settled into my consciousness. I had intentionally come to this forest—this sanctuary—hoping to find a deeper place of clarity and inspiration, and in a flash it arrived. I revisited my first dreamtime voyage experience of the vibrating, rainbow-colored light lines that connect everything, and came to understand that all of the interconnections I had been seeking were embedded in that experience.

Now it was time to pull the pieces together into a process, a map, for conscious soul evolution. I'd been working with the rainbow lights throughout my life. They had been there as a constant source of inspiration and wisdom, calling me to evolve as I lived life—coming into partnership with my husband, pursuing my education, launching my career, opening to the transformational opportunities of a significant health challenge when I was diagnosed with multiple sclerosis (MS), learning to be truly present through the heart-expanding process of raising a child, and experiencing the deep sadness of caring for aging parents in significant decline. I had stepped into the whirling rainbow lights many times, both difficult and joyful.

This time, in the embrace of the redwoods, when I stepped into the stream of consciousness of the luminous portal of light, I saw thirteen strands of light—thirteen spiritual gifts woven together into the fabric of soul. The pieces I'd been working with for many years came together into a guiding pathway—a map—for the conscious evolution of soul, with its starting point being the spiritual gifts of the rainbow lights.

What Happened on These Light Journeys?

There are many ways that one might describe the experience of my first encounter, and subsequent encounters, with the gateway or portal of light: a dreamtime vision, a transcendental voyage to another realm, or in the language of author Joseph Chilton Pearce, an experience of breaking through "the crack in the cosmic egg."[1]

I have come to understand these experiences as direct encounters with the light of *Spirit*—the source of creation permeating all. These encounters have shifted my consciousness, all of what I *know*, and launched my soul's evolution in this lifetime. They have filled me with the knowing that each of us has a spiritual gift that is an entryway to the evolution of soul—soul being the light and consciousness of Spirit fused into a coherent beam of light through the cycles of life and death. As soul we contain each one of the thirteen gifts of what I have come to call the Rainbow Wheel. We move through different stages of evolution with these gifts of higher consciousness: *The Light of Creation. Beauty. Gratitude. Breath. Ascension. Compassion. Unity. Harmony. Joy. Coherence. Peace. Love. Grace.*

My first childhood experience opened me, and it helped prepare me to eventually *consciously* evolve—to intentionally choose to direct my *intention* and *attention* to this endeavor. At times, however, especially in my youth, it felt like a burden. I didn't quite know how to speak about what I was experiencing, since the language of the times didn't provide a forum for having such conversations, at least not within my circles of family and friends. I had difficulty finding ways to talk about this encounter with the light. I didn't know how to describe the wise, guiding presence in the ray of light, as I was transported to the even more expansive presence of the portal of cosmic light. In fact, I only confided in one friend during my adolescence about this experience, and then again in my early twenties upon meeting my husband.

As my husband and I began to seek out others with whom we could deeply share the spiritual journey, we eventually connected with other people open to the possibility of such encounters. Over the years we've formed amazing circles of friends—communities based in Spirit and heart. I've read, talked with people, and sought experiences that would inform and ground me in the wisdom of the many others that have preceded me on this path of soul evolution. Through meditation I've journeyed to the gateway or portal of the Rainbow Wheel and opened my heart to *knowing*, to accessing the wisdom of Spirit, creation, and soul.

Other powerful life experiences have also nudged me toward more deeply attending to my spiritual life, such as the birth of our son, which immersed me in a completely new state of love. Attending to the care and life of this soul was a profound experience that created a new yearning to pay attention more deeply to my spiritual life. The precious nature of life crystallized before me as never before. Although I had directly experienced the light of creation, it was time to more fully engage the energy, gifts, and grace of the luminous portal of light—to open more fully to the amazing beauty of life. Creation had my attention in a new way.

As this new awareness grew within me I decided to create a ceremonial space for myself to officially mark this shift of intention and attention. I went to a peaceful place away from the sounds of civilization, sat on a huge boulder, and stated my intention and my gratitude for life. I cried a deep cry of release of all of the pent-up energy from the years of not having fully lived my knowing of the interconnectedness of all of life, for having lived outside my center. And I vowed to live life now from my center for as many moments as possible.

I stated my intention to evolve, to move through the next turn of my spiraling path, and to *consciously be* Spirit and soul here in my human form. Notifying myself, and the cosmos, seemed to bring new synchronicity to my life. People, experiences, written resources, and opportunities just seemed to appear. Wise guidance came from unexpected places. I kept responding by taking in as much as I could in each given moment so that I could learn, grow, and evolve.

As my evolutionary path unfolded, I felt a new pull to focus my attention on the support of others also intending to consciously evolve. Although I had been sharing my discoveries with friends and family, I began also to see people in individual sessions to assist them in finding their evolutionary pathways, and opening more fully into their spiritual lives.

Building upon what I had gained from my investigations and journeying, along with my experience as an educator and a facilitator of change processes for growth and development, I began helping others to formulate pathways for soul evolution—the work of stepping through gateways of change, applying one's new understandings, and engaging in spiritual practice for the purpose of conscious soul evolution.

Wondering and Opening

As I've searched for greater understanding about conscious soul evolution, I've learned that many people—in addition to the more well-known prophets and sages of the world's religions and traditions—have experienced, spoken, and written about their peak spiritual encounters and the work of moving through stages of growth. They've talked about the type of blissful experience I had in my youth when I encountered that all-knowing consciousness and presence. Philosopher Ervin Lazlo, in *Science and the Akashic Field*, reports that people in deep, altered states of consciousness "describe what they experience as an immense and unfathomable field of consciousness endowed with infinite intelligence and creative power. The field of cosmic consciousness they experience is a cosmic emptiness—a void. Yet, paradoxically, it is also an essential fullness ... It is pregnant with the possibility of everything there is."[2]

So what is happening when one encounters this cosmic consciousness? There are many views addressing this question, and many levels at which the question can be answered. Psychologist Jean Houston says that when we reach these states, we go "beyond the bandwidth of local perception and memory" and enter "a field of knowing in which much larger information can be accessed via the quantum hologram."[3] In other words, we find a way to tap into a stream of knowing that permeates the entire cosmos.

When I step into the light of the Rainbow Wheel and its consciousness I have a sense of expansion. Its energies reach out to embrace and cradle me as I go beyond the "bandwidth" of my ordinary state, and tap into more of the "unfathomable field" of cosmic consciousness. Words from the ecstatic poet Rumi eloquently capture the powerful pull of my journey that night of my youth, and since then:

How could the soul not take flight
when from the glorious presence
A soft call flows sweet as honey, comes right up to her
And whispers, "Rise up now, come away."[4]

The accounts of others, and the uplifting words of poets and other writers have helped to inform me and broaden my understanding. In the process, I've also tapped into an exciting, ongoing, informative, and dynamic global conversation about soul, and conscious evolution. I participate by reading and listening to the words of others, and also by offering my own words to the threads of this conversation. I am, in this book, telling the story that has come to me as I have expanded into this field of cosmic consciousness, grounding my learning here in my human form.

This story involves utilizing a state that is similar to that of deep meditation. It is what some refer to as a nonordinary, or altered, state of consciousness—a state outside the realm of what we consider to be normal daily life. As I connect with this stream of consciousness and the presence of this portal of light, my heart space opens. I feel a sense of wonder and then expand into an almost unimaginably deep love. It is as if I have stepped into a rain shower of light, in which each of the droplets or particles of light contains a packet of information that I open and translate into words, visual images, feelings, and knowings.

Before going any further it is important to say that I believe the process I have just described incorporates the common capacity many people refer to as their "intuition." At times, we intuitively know who is calling us when the phone rings, or we sense when someone is staring at us even though they are behind us and we have to turn around to catch them in the act. These types of occurrences are commonplace, as is documented in the research findings by British developmental biologist Rupert Sheldrake in many of his publications.

How does this information come to you? What is happening when you "sense" that a close friend is in need and you give her a call or drop by to find out how she is, only to discover she was thinking of you and needed your help? Perhaps this phenomenon is somehow related to what parapsychology researcher Dean Radin in *Entangled Minds*, describes as *entanglement*—a term that comes from the field of quantum theory. Radin says that entanglement refers to particles that are connected regardless of distance: "These connections are instantaneous, operating 'outside' the usual flow of time. They imply that at very deep levels, the separations that we see between ordinary, isolated objects are, in a sense, illusions created by our limited perceptions."[5]

Perhaps as a result of entanglement we are able to tap into streams of consciousness regularly and unpack information from the particles of those streams, thereby *knowing* who is calling or that a friend is in need. Over the years, I've been paying attention to, practicing, and cultivating this common ability that we each have. I am now able to employ it to support my evolution. And as I have worked with the information acquired in the stream of consciousness of the portal of light, I have come to understand that my work here is *to anchor the awareness of the gifts of the shimmering rainbow lights of creation.*

Sharing with you what I have been able to glean, over time, from this portal of light is part of this anchoring work—the work of bringing the gifts of the rainbow lights of creation into their fullness here in human form, into the activities and ways of daily life. In the silence of the ray of light of that first journey, I could almost "hear" an invitation, a soundless beckoning, to anchor the vibrant energy of the rainbow lights. My sense of that invitation continues to be compelling.

During my initial dream vision I peered down at the earth from above and saw a matrix of rainbow lines of light—an array of intersecting lines connecting all of creation, weaving together to form life. From this higher place of seeing and knowing, I saw the immense beauty of earth and of all of life. In an instant my heart was transformed.

Many people have reported such profound occurrences with a cosmic beam of light, for example, as written about in the literature on "near-death experiences." People report coming back from this light with a new sense of the unity of all, the love embedded in all of creation, and with a knowing of themselves as a form of this light and love. Many have reported completely changing their lives to reflect their new sense of purpose—changing their work, the offerings they make to others, and how they simply go about the daily tasks associated with living life.

My first portal journey left me with a wealth of images and sensings about the shimmering rainbow lights. I have come to see that each of these lights is a gift of creation, and that *each one of us is the embodiment of these gifts*. My work over the past twenty years has been to offer to others, one conversation at a time, what I have glimpsed in my momentary and yet infinite experiences of the pulsating, shimmering lights of creation. This has transformed my consciousness, the transcendent nature of life bursting forth upon me, igniting my unfolding journey and embrace of soul. Rumi captures the impact of this journey with these words:

What is Soul? Consciousness.
The more awareness, the deeper the soul,
and when such essence overflows, you feel a sacredness around.[6]

This sacred journey has cycles. My own process has had many types of "moments" throughout its continuing course: exhilarating, frustrating, joyful, frightening, disorienting, and miraculous. Each of these types of moments is part of the cycle of conscious soul evolution. Their rich variety can crack open spiritual states, allowing you to reach new thresholds and launching you into your next stage of unfurling life's possibilities.

The portals, or gateways, of the Rainbow Wheel provide a supporting path for you to move through such moments, phases, and cycles as you live an evolving life in the world, coming to *be*. Scholar and poet Coleman Barks describes such processes as a journey of connecting with "the deep being I've *met*, and not become."[7]

The Rainbow Wheel offers a path for meeting more of that "deep being" and coming to *be*—living the full presence of the "deep being" here, now. As you come to know and *be your* spiritual gift, you unfold, bringing your presence and the transcendent nature of the originating energy of Spirit into form.

Conscious evolution harnesses the full power of *intention* and *attention* to offer the soul what it seeks—evolution for the sake of evolution. Through evolving we are creating for the sake of creation. And in the search for this "deep being" in form, we are *collectively* gaining the capacity to consciously evolve. We stand in an incredible moment of amazing accessibility to the information, stories, energies, and practices of so many of the world's spiritual and religious traditions. It is your time to sculpt your evolutionary pathway, and it is our time to share with each other our understandings, insights, and questions about soul and consciousness.

I offer my work with the Rainbow Wheel to the circle of this collective inquiry, hopeful that what I've glimpsed—my inklings of understanding—will in some small way contribute to your journey into the shimmering light of essence overflowing. *May you "feel a sacredness around."*

2

The Story of the Rainbow Wheel

I have come to refer to the total body of information that I have unpacked from the particles of cosmic light as the Rainbow Wheel. The core focus of this information—this story—is that each of us contains and embodies all of the gifts of the whirling rainbow lights of creation. The thirteen gifts, once again, are:

The Light of Creation
Beauty
Gratitude
Breath
Ascension
Compassion
Unity
Harmony
Joy
Coherence
Peace
Love
Grace

As you identify and consciously work with your spiritual gift (Chapter 4 offers a guided meditation to help you discover your gift), I encourage you to explore the following questions as you move through the many stages, over time, of *being* your gift:

- What is the nature of this gift?

- What do I *know* about this gift?
- How can I fully *be* my gift?
- What might propel my evolution?
- How might my conscious journey of being my gift impact the evolution of others?
- How might being my gift affect my offerings to the world and to the cosmos?

My hope is that something from my story, from what I have experienced and learned about the gifts of the rainbow lights of creation, will resonate for you and support your exploration—your journey. The Rainbow Wheel is a pathway for the conscious evolution of soul, and its map offers ways of taking this journey of the light. It is one thread of the web of possible frameworks for the unfoldment of soul and the evolution of the collective. This story that I offer to you comes from my embrace of the Rainbow Wheel, which has been a source of inspiration. Perhaps something in this story will inspire you.

Many people are telling each other stories about spiritual experiences that have been important to them. Ralph Metzner, in his book *The Unfolding Self*, says that mystical experiences are more prevalent than previously thought. He writes that the *New York Times* reported on a survey of a sample of 1,500 "normal," middle-class Americans. In that survey, "Forty percent of the respondents answered affirmatively to the question 'Have you ever had the feeling of being very close to a powerful spiritual force that seemed to lift you out of yourself?' ... People who have these kinds of experiences may not know what they are or how to talk about them, but they agree that the experience is powerful, sometimes devastating, and invariably life-transforming."[1] I have, throughout my work, been privileged to hear such stories.

In addition to this global phenomenon of story sharing, there are workshops and lectures being offered worldwide by people from many different spiritual traditions and faiths to help us with this type of awareness. And researchers and thought leaders from diverse fields of study that are associated with many different institutes, centers, and universities are studying many types of spiritual experiences, states of consciousness, and insights about the nature of life and the cosmos. They are continually presenting us with new opportunities for learning.

There is also a growing awareness of the spiritual lives of children. Parents, educators, researchers, artists, and counselors of many types are coming together to explore how to nurture the spiritual development of our youth, and to hear our children as they speak their own powerful insights. Having been a child who had an extraordinary experience, I feel this is especially important. I was blessed that my mother's response to the telling of my story was kind, loving, and allowing.

Although she could not see what I was seeing, my mother's acceptance of me was crucial to paving the way for my continued evolution. Now, as we are gathering and giving voice to insights and perspectives arising from a variety of fields of study, we seem to be finding new ways of understanding such extraordinary experiences and their potential contributions to the conscious evolution of soul and society.

For me, this journey of the *extra*ordinary began in this lifetime during that summer night of my youth. Although I refer to my experience as "*extra*ordinary," perhaps my greatest learning has been to come to know this sensibility of the extraordinary as my everyday experience of the miracle of life. That, I believe, is a significant part of the evolutionary process—recognizing this capacity to experience the extraordinary, and then bringing it into greater presence each day of life.

What Is Transformation?

Consciousness researcher Ralph Metzner, in his book *The Unfolding Self*, reminds us that "our experience confirms what the elders and wise ones of all times have said—that we live in a state of constant change … We grow up … we grow old … but we always grow."[2] Throughout life we go through many types of experiences, transitions, and stages. Some are the "normal" changes of life that we've come to expect in our society—relocating, job changes, marriage and partnership, divorce, births, and deaths.

Others are outside this realm—they are usually unexpected, and we are generally less rehearsed in dealing with them. Some of these fall into the category that Metzner refers to as "another kind of transformation, a radical restructuring of the entire psyche that has been variously referred to as mystical experience, ecstasy, cosmic consciousness, oceanic feeling, oneness, transcendence, union with God, nirvana, satori, liberation, peak experience, and by other names."[3]

The world's spiritual traditions and mystics across time have spoken to us about the process of such radical restructuring or transformation, about what it is and how one might arrive at its doorstep, intentionally or otherwise. Some practices may lead to what philosopher Ken Wilber refers to as "miniature transformations" that prepare you for more radical transformations and restructuring such that you know that "there is only the enlightened mind wherever you look."[4]

The conscious work of the Rainbow Wheel is intended to help you arrive at what Metzner refers to as a "threshold crossing"[5]—a dimension that is filled with both the familiar and the new simultaneously. These crossings are gateways to transformation. The practices of the Rainbow Wheel may help nudge you into states of heightened awareness and create miniature transformations, moving you on toward radical transformation.

Why Transform and Evolve?

There is an impulse, a drive that comes from deep within each of us. It is the creative growth cycle of life imprinted in the light and consciousness of our souls, and in all of the particles of stardust—in all of the matter—that comprise our human forms. This cycle can be activated in many ways, such as was the case with my powerful childhood experience, or through subtler and quieter ways, perhaps while taking a walk in a favorite park or watching children play. It comes from an energy force that derives from the very pattern of creation itself: the cycle of growth that is in all of us.

We are wired to bring soul to the next level and to offer evolution to all of creation. It is me creating creation, and you creating creation. This is me—all of the levels of "me"—generating life, and "you" generating life. As far as I can tell, nothing else is possible. I may temporarily fool myself into thinking I can just stand still, but, really, I can't. I'll have to move at some point—if not in this lifetime, then the next, or the next one after that.

The creation pattern within me dictates that this is so. *Spirit ... God ... the Absolute ... Great Spirit ... the Great Ultimate ... Divine Source*—this is what is embedded within, what I breathe into my being from the air around me, and what I absorb from the light of the sun. This sacred creation pattern is the very essence of my nature, so I create. Indeed, researcher Roger Walsh, in his study of the "perennial philosophy" of the world's cultures, traditions, and religions, has found a common understanding that we are "eternally and intimately linked"[6] to the sacred. This link to the sacred propels evolution, *for the sake of evolution*—we are creating, *for the sake of creation*.

For me, the push to evolve in this lifetime has been present since I encountered the whirling vortex of light. It was as if that experience activated some component of my DNA—like a computer program that was waiting to be called up. And once this program was initiated, there was no going back. Well, not permanently anyway.

I did go through phases of actually trying very hard *not* to pay attention to my evolution, to this DNA program or its impulses and signals, sometimes out of fear and at other times out of simply not knowing how to proceed. But then something would happen—an experience, an insight, or the gift of the wisdom of another—and I just couldn't help myself! A powerful love would call to me and

I had to go. While I don't know where this might lead—this grand mystery of life—I am very grateful to be along for this incredible ride, hopeful that my creating creation will be of service.

Three Strategies to Cultivate Courage

Courage is needed as you consciously evolve and reveal yourself to yourself. As you leap through gateways you can release physical, mental, emotional, and ego patterns for the sake of the evolution of your soul. You can release the moorings that you have constructed and woven. Layers, familiar and perhaps even previously useful, can drop away, allowing you to soar into a new stage of being, opening new possibilities for life as you embrace the gifts of the rainbow lights of creation within you.

Illusions, useful as they might have once been for keeping a certain order, are exposed and comfort zones are left behind, and that takes courage. Many different and sometimes disturbing emotions can surface to be released in this dance of letting go—*dying to yourself*—and then launching yourself into spiritual rebirth. As you come to more fully *be* your spiritual gift and walk through its entryway to evolution, you may also find yourself coming face-to-face with uncomfortable realizations about certain aspects of yourself and your life. And you may find that change, even desired change, is sometimes challenging. Courage helps you move through these transitions and transformations of soul evolution, guiding you to reach for new growth and unleashing your wise, inspired self to come fully forward for this awe-filled venture of *being* creation.

This phase of evolution—this work of dying to yourself—is sometimes referred to as "the dark night of the soul." Christopher Bache, professor of religious studies, describes this as a stage "in which our identity as a discrete self is challenged at its core and ultimately surrendered."[7] When you connect with the cosmos, with creation, in a fundamentally new way, allowing yourself to see connections, relationships, and the wholeness and unity of life through a new lens, you may find that you no longer see *yourself* in the same way either.

You could experience a sense of deconstruction. This, however, frees you to immerse yourself in a new sense of wonderment, allowing you to glide into the formation of new patterns of life that fully support the creation pattern within. Use your courage to keep a sense of balance and wholeness, nurturing and caring for yourself and those that are joining you in the dance of life. Remember, your work will affect others, and having the courage to be gentle with yourself and those around you will bring greater ease to this process.

Courage gives you momentum to do this work, a running start that lifts you from the comfort you have felt in your knowing of you. It may feel as though you are hurtling yourself into a void. And although the void—the plenum, the ground field for life—is in reality filled with light and all possibility, the journey can feel, at times, like you are crossing a deep, dark abyss. Your practices and self-care will help you make these leaps. This is truly a journey of both joyful and hard work. Have the courage to push yourself to leap *and* also pace yourself, for this is truly a balancing act.

Conscious evolution requires a willingness to transform, and courage can be vital for this work, supporting you to engage your willingness, and to follow practices that guide and ground you so that you can move into the next stage of your evolution. There are three strategies, in particular, for cultivating and nurturing courage that have been significant for me: invoking, connecting, and releasing. The first strategy, *invoking a field of higher consciousness* (for example, *Love*), infuses me with a sense of my larger potentiality and inspires me to gather and use courage. This strategy, which is fundamental to the Rainbow Wheel process, will be described throughout the book beginning in Chapter 3. It has been key for me in cultivating courage, and it also has other significant potential benefits for soul evolution.

The second strategy has been to *connect with others and share my journey*. Even one or two such connections at different times had a tremendous impact on cultivating and nurturing my capacity for summoning courage. Knowing that I stand in the company of others as I do my evolutionary work has fortified my courage.

The third strategy has been a practice of *examining and releasing energies* that restrict my knowing of the creation pattern within me. Sometimes I can name them—like fear or doubt—and other times it's simply a feeling, like a heavy pit in the bottom of my stomach. As I've become aware of them I've swirled those energies together into a bundle and suspended them in midair. This act allows me to then step back (since I have, at least momentarily, become untangled from them, or at least less tangled than previously), so that I might examine their history with me over time. I might ask: What is this fear about? Why has it surfaced now? What is its origin? What effect does it have? How do I participate with it and why? Then, after spending time in this state of examination, I send these energies back out into the void of creation, with gratitude and love, to be transformed for the benefit of all.

This has taken courage, this process of noticing, examining, and releasing energies that I've been carrying with me for decades or even lifetimes. And even though in that present moment I may have come to know them as energies that are interfering with the evolution of my soul, it can be a rattling experience to let them go. Invoking a field of higher consciousness, such as *Love*, helps me to remember my true divine nature and to surrender all else that is not. Through this process of releasing I have been building courage and practicing the art of summoning it forth for soul evolution.

Sri Aurobindo, the founder of Integral Yoga, is quoted as having said that "the development of spiritual consciousness is an exceedingly vast and complex affair in which all sorts of things can happen and one might almost say that for each man it is different according to his nature and that the one thing that is essential is the inner call and aspiration and the perseverance to follow always after it, no matter how long it takes, what are the difficulties or impediments, because nothing else will satisfy the soul within us."[8]

Courage may very likely be needed at various points along your unfolding pathway. You may find that, at first, initiating a conscious evolutionary process is more of a leap than a calculated calling forth of courage. Many, including myself, speak of a sense of having *had* to initiate this journey. As was the case with me, there may have even been a spontaneous experience that created a sense of being in an expansive, cosmic state that just *had* to be explored.

Looking back, it may not feel as though courage was actually needed, at least not at the beginning; there may simply have been a knowing that the leap *needed* to be made. It wasn't the type of choice such as waking up in the morning and asking yourself whether or not you'll have a cup of coffee, but rather a choice along the lines of asking yourself, "Shall I take a breath this morning?" You don't ask the question; you just do it because a deep and driving force compels you.

You may find that you *must* begin this journey because of an inner call, or an experience may occur that simply pulls you into a new state of consciousness and pathway for soul evolution. Perhaps you will have a dream that shifts your consciousness and propels you into further exploration. Or you may consciously choose to initiate this process. Whichever the case, there may be many moments when courage is needed as you, according to your own nature, forge your pathway.

Rumi speaks to this task as a total exposure, no matter how you might come to it:

Take off your phenomena-clothes
When you enter the soul's steam bath: no
one comes in here with clothes on.[9]

In that initial moment, that fraction of a second in which you plunge into "the soul's steam bath" whether spontaneous or planned, courage may be necessary. I have needed to find courage all along, releasing and coming to understand fear and doubt, and forging ahead with hopefulness. The process of the Rainbow Wheel map has helped me with this task by providing strategies for gaining the courage to continue. Throughout the book, I offer information that is intended to support you in accessing courage as you make your way along this unfolding pathway.

As you evolve, courage will help you allow yourself to be present and continue on, while what you have previously known as "you" changes. Courage may be needed to keep opening new gateways for creating "you." It can also support you in committing to the practices needed for your continuing evolution—practices that will cultivate this capacity to evolve. This is an act of choosing, of engaging your willingness and courage for the sake of the evolution of your soul, and for all of creation. Rumi reminds us:

There's courage involved if you want to become truth.[10]

Stepping into the Stream

Throughout the book I have incorporated lines from the poems of Jelaluddin Rumi (1207–73). According to Rumi scholar Coleman Barks, Rumi was born in a region of the Persian empire that is now part of Afghanistan, and later settled in what is now Turkey. He was a devout scholar and directed the study of "theology, poetry, music, and other subjects and practices related to the growth of the soul."[11] Rumi was part of a community and tradition that "was open to the heart, to explore the mystery of union, to fiercely search for and try to say truth, and to celebrate the glory and difficulty of being in a human incarnation."[12]

Barks tell us that Rumi's volumes of poems and discourses were based on his inquiry about the higher purposes, meanings, dreams, and visions of human life, as well as from the practical questions of living life. Rumi was part of a community of people in the working world, not those renouncing daily life, and so the questions he explored involved both cosmic and practical, daily life.

Words can create streams, and I have found a stream in Rumi's poems that has helped me give voice to the Rainbow Wheel vision and story of conscious soul evolution. The lines I have selected come from the words of Rumi translators and scholars Coleman Barks, Andrew Harvey, and Shahram Shiva.

My hope is that the stream created by Rumi's words will help carry you along, provide insight, and guide understanding. There's a long, deep tradition of scholarship and study involving Rumi's massive works. I have chosen just a few of the many lines of his poetry, as translated by others, to help convey the essence of the Rainbow Wheel. May these words clarify, uplift, entice, inspire, and deepen your understanding.

Three Strategies to Support Your Evolutionary Work

The work of conscious soul evolution is joyful and often rapturous, and it is also definitely *work*. It requires great intention, attention, and care. It requires you to use every faculty—intelligence, imagination, feeling, sensing, and knowing. Everything is used in a heightened state of awareness. Everything is in play. Your full self is needed for the evolutionary journey. Rumi urges us to do this work when he says:

Keep your intelligence white-hot
and your grief glistening, so your
life will stay fresh.[13]

We work using the sharp edges of our intelligence, feeling all and joyfully reveling in the freshness of life. Conscious evolution is a flowing process of letting go and receiving. This is a cycle. Letting go—suspending, surrendering, emptying out, purifying in the fire of life—is work. The intention of the Rainbow Wheel process is to support you, with gentleness and ease, in this cycle of letting go and receiving. This is a continually unfolding picture, with changes at every turn. Like with a kaleidoscope, you look through the lens and see a beautiful pattern; then when you turn it everything changes, and a new, even more beautiful pattern is formed.

As you take on this work of conscious evolution, create a vision of yourself in this dance of challenge *and* joy—a vision of you growing and evolving, and becoming the sweet nectar of life. Gather together carefully chosen circles of supporting resources to embrace, assist, and guide you. This may include friends and family, therapists and counselors, healers, energyworkers, bodyworkers, meditation guides, yoga instructors, dance and movement instructors, and writing and art professionals.

Read books that you are drawn to, journal about life—both your daytime and your dreamtime lives. The Rainbow Wheel is intended to enhance your other ongoing evolutionary resources and supports, but not replace them. Broadly engage the resources of your life, including the Rainbow Wheel, and weave a network of support for the evolution of your soul.

You may find Ken Wilber's "Integral Life Practice Matrix,"[14] in *Integral Spirituality*, to be of assistance in formulating your evolutionary practices.

Support and care for yourself. Evolution is a challenging process of opening fully to *being* the deep divine within, in your human physical form. You may gain some profound new insights that lead you to enact changes in your world and how you live life. Caring for yourself is very important so that you can be in a state of wholeness and ease, uplifting yourself even as you traverse what may seem like difficult transitions. Conscious evolution may not be an "easy" process, but it is a process that can be enacted from a state of flow and filled with grace. When we engage all of ourselves, we "stay fresh" and open to new possibilities and gateways.

To help facilitate your evolutionary work process, in addition to your other circles of supporting resources, I have incorporated three strategies throughout the book: *stories*, *meditations*, and *practices*. The first strategy is stories. Throughout time, we have told each other stories to help guide and inform our work. They let us know that others have gone before us on this pathway and provide a way of sharing the wisdom that has been harvested. The second strategy uses meditations. They nudge us into spaces we might not otherwise go, opening some of the gateways to our deeper selves. Finally, the third strategy of practices offers avenues for anchoring your new awareness, helping it to take hold within and launching the next phase of your evolutionary cycle. My hope is that these stories, meditations, and practices will enrich your journey:

Stories. There are stories throughout the book that are meant to illustrate the Rainbow Wheel information in action and the many ways that evolution can occur. While these stories are fictional, they are based on and incorporate my own personal learning and insights from my work with others. They are meant to illustrate the wide range of ways the Rainbow Wheel evolutionary process might manifest in a person's life; the stories are also a reminder that even with a map in hand you are creating your own pathway.

Meditations. The meditations provided are guiding experiences that invite you to the deepest inner realms of yourself so that you can access and explore your highest wisdom and knowing. These meditations are offered as ways for connecting with yourself and with creation's fields of higher consciousness. Each meditation is based on the first one that you will encounter in Chapter 4. That meditation, *The Clear Light of the Heart*, is used as the guiding format for the remaining meditations. While much of that meditation is the same each time it appears, there are also important differences. The meditation is repeated in its entirety each time it is offered. Meditation is a way of connecting with your deepest self and inviting its knowing and inspiration more fully into your conscious life.

Practices. Practices for integrating and expanding your evolutionary work are suggested. They are intended to support you in more fully embracing your evolution and changes in consciousness. The integrating practices help you merge with your experiences as fully as you can, bringing that knowing into form. This is a way we progress—by fully taking it all in at a deep level. When we listen to a musician perform a piece from memory, and watch him sway and lift off in his ecstatic delight and sheer joy of the sounds, we are witnessing the musician *as* the music. And the musician got there, to that place of integration and being the music, through practice. It is as if practice transformed the cells of his very being, allowing him to become the music—total integration. Through your spiritual practice, *you* become *you*.

The practices sections also include reflective questions for your inner exploration, as well as questions for small-group conversation. This inner reflection is an important part of a conscious evolutionary process. And further, as we sit together in community, we can tap our collective wisdom and create together. The practices provided throughout the book fall into three categories:

- *Integrating Practices*—practices to support embracing, anchoring, and integrating the effects of conscious soul evolution.

- *Inquiry Practices—Individual Reflection*: reflective questions to help you to clarify where you are and what is needed in the present moment for your evolution.

- *Sacred Circle Practices—Collective Reflection*: questions for tapping your inner wisdom and the collective wisdom of others on a path of conscious soul evolution. There are many useful formats for calling sacred circles together for the purpose of collective, sacred reflection and dialogue. More will be said about this in Chapter 5.

At the end of the book you'll find an additional list of resources to support your evolutionary work. Given that there is a vast wealth of written materials spanning centuries of evolutionary work to help guide the process, these suggestions are offered as a very small sampling of the available wisdom and guidance.

Your Sacred Journey

The journey of evolving soul is sacred, and you have a gift that is a key to taking this sacred voyage. Really, you not only *have* a gift, you *are* a gift, a gem of creation. You are, in essence, the keeper of your spiritual gift. And just as shopkeepers tend to the well-being of their shops, you can tend to the well-being of your spiritual gift so that your soul evolves. As previously indicated, at the end of each chapter practices will be presented that can support your work. The first practice offered in this book is an integrating practice focused on remembering—remembering that you are here on a soul voyage and that you are already evolving. Now you are being invited to travel farther along this unfolding, spiraling corridor of life.

Practices for Conscious Soul Evolution

Integrating Practices—practices to support embracing, anchoring, and integrating the effects of conscious soul evolution.

• Telling One of Your Soul Evolution Stories

I began this book by sharing with you one of my soul evolution stories—the story of an experience that profoundly affected my consciousness, and shaped my life and my soul. We all have soul experiences that have shaped us, prodded us along a certain pathway, nudged us to live life in certain ways, enticed us into wondering about the cosmos and the nature of life, or supplied us with glimpses that have changed our view of life.

Our stories may be long or short, subtle or stark, specific or broad. They may encompass wondrous or spectacular experiences, "ah-ha" moments, or insights hard-won from the work of living life. Remembering our stories, whatever types they may be, helps bring our evolutionary pathways to a new level of consciousness. Through telling our stories to ourselves, and to others, we become more conscious of our soul path.

Author Christina Baldwin writes, "Story is the song line of a person's life. We need to sing it and we need someone to hear the singing. Story told, story heard, story written, story read create the web of life in words."[15] I invite you to remember one of *your* soul evolution stories—a story from your life in which you experienced soul in a new way, one that affected you and your life. Think about how you viewed life and soul before the event or the emerging insights, and then after. Tell yourself this story by writing it, and then share the story with another person.

Invite that person to be what Baldwin refers to as a "storycatcher," someone who "invoke[s] the invisible basket of time and attention that holds story."[16] By telling the story to another, you increase the power of what was learned—what you came to know through this story, and what becomes known by another. As Baldwin says, "Story couples our experiences, mind to mind and heart to heart."[17]

So, what is one of *your* soul evolution stories?

3

The Rainbow Wheel Map for Conscious Soul Evolution

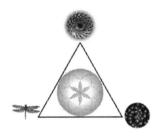

When I step into the stream of light of the Rainbow Wheel portal, I translate the particles of energy of that light into words and visual images. I open to the wisdom and knowing of those particles of light. It is as if I am reading a book, looking through the illustrations, taking in the words, and opening to the meanings offered to me by the author. I am searching for the highest and richest view I can access from my current stage of evolution.

These "translations" and interpretations are mine—they come through the filter of the lens of "me" in my totality, from my life experiences and my evolutionary stage. Others reading this same portal book might have different insights. In many ways this is similar to a book group—everyone reads the same book, and then the group comes together to share unique translations, insights, and understandings, each from their own place on their life path. In this particular case, I have been "reading" the book of this luminous portal of the Rainbow Wheel and sharing my understanding of it with others. These translations and insights have been informed by my life experiences, my studies, my work with other people, and where I am, overall, in this evolutionary process. I have attempted, as well, to ground these translations and interpretations by learning from the wisdom of others.

These translations have formed a map for conscious soul evolution. Maps illustrate pathways for many types of journeys, and they can come to us in many different forms. The Rainbow Wheel map for conscious soul evolution, illustrated in Figure 1 and in color on the back cover, has four portals or gateways that can assist you in consciously unfolding your soul's evolution. The portals comprise a way of launching yourself farther along the pathway of coming to *be* the deep, divine you, interconnected to the whole of the cosmos.

Figure 1.
The Rainbow Wheel Map
for Conscious Soul Evolution

Overview of the Portals

Following is a brief overview of the transformational work of each of the four portals. In the chapters that follow, this description will be elaborated upon and specific suggestions for working with each portal will be offered.

Portal One: *Invoking Your Spiritual Gift*

You have a primary spiritual gift that is a key to opening new gateways and is an entryway for conscious soul evolution. The thirteen gifts of the Rainbow Wheel, illustrated in Figure 2 and in color on the front cover, are among the highest resonances of creation, each with its own layers. These fields of higher consciousness are intense and powerful vibrations that ultimately can align your energy field with creation's pure, clear light.

Figure 2.
The Rainbow Wheel
Spiritual Gifts and Color Vibrations

The Light of Creation—Golden
Beauty—Yellow
Gratitude—Green
Breath—Cobalt Blue
Ascension—Indigo Blue
Compassion—Deep Purple

Unity—Violet/Lavender
Harmony—Red
Joy—Magenta/Pink
Coherence—Orange
Peace—Ultraviolet
Love—White
Grace—Clear Light

Invoking, which is the act of intentionally calling or summoning forth, is central to further initiating the evolution of your soul. This is an act of *choice* that, in a range of forms and called by different names, has always been part of our religious and spiritual traditions. Invoking the many dimensions of your primary gift, or of any of these gifts of higher consciousness, can initiate a new phase of evolution. Invoking your gift infuses and uplifts you with the sublime magnificence of these lights of creation. There are also color vibrations associated with the gifts that assist you in amplifying your work with your gift (Chapter 5 provides further information about the color vibrations). Through bathing in this light, your energy field begins to match this higher vibration. As this vibration of higher consciousness flows through and surrounds you, new possibilities for your evolution emerge.

Portal Two: *Liberating the Gatekeepers*
As you live life, many different types of energies, both internal and external, vie for your attention. Some can support evolution, for example, energies associated with an impulse to create. Others, such as a sense that you "aren't good enough," can interfere with evolution because these energies *distort* the clarity of the creation pattern within.

Underlying these distorting energies is a root or core distortion, which is an energy pattern that is incessantly disruptive to your evolution. It fragments and disrupts your life force energy, which has a disorienting effect, pulling you away from your divine center. You might think of it as the proverbial pea under the mattress; even if your body finds a way to get used to it, your underlying consciousness always knows that it is there because it continually feels and is impacted by the disruptive affects to your state of wholeness.

The core distortion is surrounded and encapsulated by habits—gatekeepers—that keep this energy pattern locked in place, much like an energy blockade. Habits create a fog of illusion that keeps the core distortion hidden from your view and awareness. If you do not know about the existence of the core distortion, changing it is more challenging. The habits are acting as gatekeepers of the status quo, keeping a certain rhythm to your life, obscuring the possibility of change, and preventing a deeper knowing of your divine self. These gatekeepers can manifest as a wide range of emotional, mental, and behavioral patterns.

The work of the Rainbow Wheel is focused on the energy level underlying the habits. Placing your intention and attention on invoking your spiritual gift, while also mindfully examining your core distortion, can energetically liberate these gatekeepers, allowing the energy of the core distortion to dissipate. This has a restorative effect upon your energy field. The image of the dragonfly, illustrated in Figure 3, is used in the Rainbow Wheel map to signify that this second portal transforms illusions. Dragonfly has been used over time as a metaphor for lifting the veils of illusion.

Invoking the vibration of the field of higher consciousness of your spiritual gift, such as *Peace* or *Joy*, assists in the process of liberating these gatekeepers, transforming the illusions they have created, and opening new possibilities for coming to be your deep, divine self. This process is referred to as "liberation" because the energies of the gatekeepers are free once again to rejoin the void of creation, and to become available as light energy moving on to create. And as a result of this conscious evolutionary process you have the opportunity to become aware of new possibilities for your spiraling path.

Figure 3.
Dragonfly: Symbol for Transforming Illusions

The focus of this portal is on diffusing the underlying energy base of the core distortion and its energetic gatekeepers so that the fullness of your spiritual gift can shine throughout your entire field and fill your life.

Portal Three: *Spiraling Breath*

Breath creates a clear pathway for the energy of your spiritual gift to move through you in every direction. As you intentionally work with the sacred breath of life, spiraling it throughout all of your physical form, the energies and vibrations of your gift have an increasingly clear and unencumbered pathway. The image of the spiral, Figure 4, is used in the Rainbow Wheel map to illustrate the movement of spiraling your breath throughout your form and energy field.

Figure 4.
The Spiral: Pathways for the Breath

The sacred spiraling breath cleanses and heals your energy centers—the vortexes of spiraling energy that connect you to all light and life throughout the cosmos. Along a vertical line through the center of the body, there is a column of connected vortexes or chakras, which means wheels of light. These spiraling energy centers circulate energy throughout your body and your entire field, radiating light and energy in a never-ending exchange with the cosmos. However, by simply living life, you come in contact with a variety of lower, denser, or heavier energies—including those of the core distortion. And these vortexes can become clogged and slowed, diverted from their natural spin and rhythm. Engaging in a practice of working with the sacred breath helps to reestablish the intended flow, which then also allows the higher vibration of your gift to move through you, attuning all of you to this field of higher consciousness.

As you come to *be* your gift, your evolution unfolds. The intention of this portal of Spiraling Breath is to consciously breathe forth yourself as an evolving creation. And in doing so, to also breathe forth the evolving creation of the cosmos.

Portal Four: *Renewing the Genesis Pattern*

"The Genesis Pattern" is a term that comes from the ancient science of sacred geometry, which studies the geometrical patterns that are the foundation of life. You may be most familiar with the science of sacred geometry through its expression in the stained glass windows of the great cathedrals, such as the famous rose windows of Notre Dame and Chartres cathedrals.

The Genesis Pattern, illustrated in Figure 5, is found etched in the stones of ancient sites throughout the world. Through its pattern of interconnected spheres, it illustrates the fundamental spherical energy pattern of life.

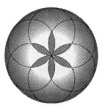

Figure 5.
The Genesis Pattern

Spiritual teacher Drunvalo Melchizedek in *The Ancient Secret of the Flower of Life*, describes the Genesis Pattern as the basic pattern of creation: "The entire fabric of everything in our existence is made up of 'marbles'—all different sizes of spheres. We're sitting on a sphere, the Earth, and spheres are rotating around us. The Moon, Sun and stars are all spheres. The whole universe, from macrocosm to microcosm, is made up of little spheres in one way or the other."[1] And so are our human bodies—we are formed from spheres dividing into more spheres. Geometrical patterns are the foundation of life. The core distortion interferes with the deep spherical creation pattern within you, causing jagged edges in its life force pattern, as illustrated in Figure 6.

Figure 6.
The Jagged Edges of the Core Distortion

Through your work with the first three portals of the Rainbow Wheel map, these jagged edges become smoother and clearer. Then, as you stand in the center of the fourth portal, you fuse with the pure ground field of life—the energy field that flows throughout all of creation. Through this process you renew and take the next step of more fully revitalizing the Genesis Pattern, the very essence of the life force energy of creation, within you. The process of the fourth portal supports you in bringing your full ***presence***—the fullness of the deep, divine being—into form.

The Story Behind the Map

The Rainbow Wheel map is based on a story—a view—of the evolutionary process. Every story, told in its own unique way, incorporates certain premises, assumptions, and understandings. The essence of the premise that underlies this particular story of the Rainbow Wheel is reflected in Rumi's words:

*You are the truth from foot to brow. Now,
what else would you like to know?* [2]

The story behind this map is one of coming to embody this knowing that you are the *truth* of the shimmering rainbow lights.

Another premise of this story is that the soul's path is that of evolution—of creation continuing to create. Through conscious intention and attention, your evolutionary pathway unfolds. Through the work of acknowledging the gift of creation within you, and clearing distorted energies, you can transcend where you are currently residing on the evolutionary spiral, transform, and move on to your next stage. Your full presence can arise as an offering to the whole of the cosmos. We have a yearning for evolution embedded in the very fabric of our beings, and it compels us to move forward, to reach and expand. Rumi reminds us that:

*We have been secretly fed
from beyond space and time. That's why we look for
something more than this.*³

Key Dimensions of the Map

The two key dimensions of this map of conscious evolution are:

• *the thirteen spiritual gifts*
• *the core distortion*

Together, they provide the guiding framework as you journey through the portals of this map, leaping along your unfolding spiral path. These dimensions will be discussed in greater detail in the remaining chapters of this book, but first I'd like to take a moment to say a few words about each one.

The Thirteen Spiritual Gifts

The cosmos is filled with energy vibrations and waves, and the Rainbow Wheel is composed of thirteen of these higher vibrations, identified previously in Figure 2. This wheel of gifts is a whirling wheel of the higher energies of the rainbow lights of creation and offers to you a full spectrum of creation's possibilities. Your energy field already contains all of these fields of higher consciousness, and like the strings on a guitar, each of these fields has its own vibrational frequency.

Since you already contain each of these vibrations within, you naturally vibrate to all of these frequencies. However, one of the frequencies—your primary gift—has a slightly stronger vibration than the others (as previously indicated, Chapter 4 offers a guided meditation experience for assisting you in identifying your gift). Often, other people already know what your gift is. Even before *you* might be paying conscious attention to your gift, others around you may detect its stronger vibration. Recognition of this will surface in conversations we have about each other. For example, you may comment that someone you know is always very compassionate. Or perhaps you notice and speak about how loving a person is toward everyone, even total strangers. A friend might offer you the reflection that you always seem to burst forth with joy. Your gift is at the core of your very nature, so others will often easily recognize it and sense its stronger vibration.

This stronger vibration is actually a "gift" in two ways. First, this field of higher consciousness, because of its strength, attracts your attention in each of your lifetimes. This vibration gets noticed and through your conscious attention you can then work to evolve it. Since all of the gifts are inextricably interwoven, any conscious attention applied to one gift ultimately affects all of them. It is like a piece of woven latticework, with light lines and energy waves intersecting everywhere.

The frequencies of all of the gifts strengthen and evolve from your work with your primary gift. At some point in your conscious evolutionary work with these fields of higher consciousness, you may begin to recognize other gifts that are vibrating with the same strength as your primary gift. Or perhaps you are already aware of this occurring. Since you brought all of your prior evolutionary work into this lifetime, it is very possible that other spiritual gifts are already matching the vibrational intensity of your primary gift.

Second, as you evolve your spiritual gift, moving to new stages of experience, insight, understanding, and *beingness*, you are offering its vibration to all. As you embody your gift in fuller form, you offer the strength of its frequency to others, opening a gateway for activating a new consciousness in those you meet. Just as with the strings of a guitar, if you pluck one string, any other object in the area with that same frequency will also begin to vibrate.

You might think of this as being like the stadium wave in which one person stands up with arms moving up and down in a wavelike motion, and then the next person does the same thing, and so on and so on, until the wave has traveled around the entire stadium. Each person is responding to the almost electric-like energy that is traveling through the crowd—we just jump up and participate. We respond to the energy.

As you strengthen your vibration, you can potentially set off the same vibration in others. If you strengthen the vibration of *Gratitude* within yourself, family members, friends, and coworkers may just find that they are feeling and offering more gratitude as well. Your work can also help attract the attention of others to the vibrations of their own spiritual gifts, opening new gateways for their evolution.

This effect is enhanced by both *invocation* and *evocation*. When working with the spiritual gifts of the Rainbow Wheel through invocation and evocation, you are calling upon or summoning forth energy. When you *invoke*, you call an energy field to come to you—to infuse you. When you *evoke*, you elicit an energy already present within. Since we have all of these vibrations of the spiritual gifts within us, the act of invoking—summoning forth—a particular energy field awakens that energy already within us as well. And your invocation, in addition to affecting you, can also touch and evoke these energies in others because of the interconnectedness of the cosmos—because of the interrelatedness of the energy waves.

When you are *consciously* working with your gift, the possibility of its offering is profoundly enhanced. This is a gift of evolution. The stronger vibration of your gift is an invitation from creation to *you* for *your* evolution. And as you heed that call, you are offering the gift of evolution to others. This is a cycle of creation. You are being invited to open to *all* of the possibilities of life and to offer these possibilities to all.

The Core Distortion

We each contend with many different energies that are part of our daily lives—relationships, world news, jobs, and a variety of encounters with different people. We develop and adopt patterns and habits to help us cope with these energies. These patterns that we take on—and they can develop over many lifetimes—impact the clarity of the energy field of the Genesis Pattern within us. These habits can create energetic interference, much like a storm interferes with radio or television reception. Jagged edges form in your energy field, as was illustrated in Figure 6.

There are many layers of habits and patterns, but ultimately underneath them all there is a core energy pattern that sustains all of the other layers. This pattern, as indicated earlier, is referred to as the **core distortion**; it is incessantly disruptive to your evolution and may have been with you for many lifetimes. It is called a distortion because it distorts the energy and shape of the Genesis Pattern within. This distortion has a fragmenting and disorienting effect on your consciousness because it interferes with the basic life force energy pattern of creation. This can manifest in a wide range of persisting emotional patterns, thought forms, and behaviors that become gatekeepers for the core distortion.

This distortion interferes with your knowing that you are individually, and we are collectively, one with creation. The core distortion is a primary energy pattern that has become embedded in your energy field and shows up in many different ways in your life, triggering a range of feelings, behaviors and responses. For example, your core energy distortion may manifest as a sense of "not being totally lovable," or "being deficient," or perhaps "not being enough." This sense may have arisen from some condition of childhood, or it may have come with you into this lifetime, becoming activated at some point. Other layers of interfering and distorted energies are connected to this primary energy pattern of the core distortion.

Upon this core distortion other distortions are built and laid until you have an entire array of energy distortions. Together, they create a web of disruptions and jagged edges in your energy field. In addition to manifesting in a variety of mental and emotional habits, the core distortion may also affect your sense of physical well-being. For example, I get a tight knot in my stomach that makes me feel shaky and ill when the energy of my core distortion is reeling. However, knowing about this core distortion allows me to bring my higher consciousness to the situation. It creates an opportunity for dissolving or dissipating it and its gatekeepers, and restoring the Genesis Pattern to its state of clarity and wholeness. I can feel the knot release when I shift my stance from one of engaging the habits of the core distortion to focusing on the energies of any of the spiritual gifts.

The purpose of identifying your core distortion is to bring your conscious attention to this energy and its multiplicity of effects on your evolution. It is a sabotaging energy. It begins for many different reasons, from many different life experiences, and may have even begun as a perceived strategy for protecting you from potential harm in this life or another. Ken Wilber in *Integral Spirituality* says that there is a "hierarchy of defenses" that is experienced *within* as fear being felt in many different ways. Wilber says we have a "threat zone" from which one will "deny, displace, repress, project, and alienate, resulting in psychological miscarriages, malformations, pain, and suffering."[4] What is important here in working with the Rainbow Wheel is not to judge the core distortion and its resulting manifestations, but to learn, transcend, transform, and evolve. You can energetically dissipate the core distortion and alleviate its continuous interference.

Exploring and learning about the specific psychological and behavioral patterns connected to the energy of your core distortion can be an important part of the evolutionary process. While engaged in this process, you may find that counseling is a vital support. As you move through the transitions and changes that can occur as a result of shifting your focus to the energy field of a higher frequency—the frequency of your spiritual gift—attend to giving yourself all of the care and support that is needed. The core distortion does manifest in many different ways, and working through its effects can, at times, be challenging. It is important to support yourself with a network of resources.

Fields of higher consciousness such as the spiritual gifts are powerful, as has been highlighted for us across the ages by prophets, spiritual leaders, and sages. When these energies are showered upon you through invocation, they can break apart and dissipate the lower energies of the core distortion. This process begins to eliminate the jagged edges of the core distortion, with fewer and fewer of these edges remaining in your field, until the original wholeness of the Genesis Pattern is once again restored, as illustrated in Figure 7.

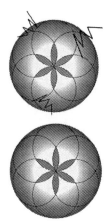

Figure 7.
Eliminating Energetic Jagged Edges
to Restore Wholeness

This energetic dissipation process often involves a type of weaving of strategies. For example, the knot in my stomach alerts me to this bundle of energy being activated, and I may become aware of a familiar message rolling round my head, attempting to take control of the situation. For me, that message might be something such as, "Keep things calm." Through shifting my attention to invoking my spiritual gift, I step away from the old, familiar message, allowing myself to be present in the moment and discern from a higher view what might actually be needed. And I now also have the opportunity, having put the old message on hold, to later examine the roots and effects of the message rolling around in my head—I can learn and transform.

Through this weaving of strategies, and with the assistance of the invocational field of your spiritual gift, your evolution can then once again unfold, unimpeded, and follow its own natural rhythm and flow.

Where Does This Path Lead?

This path of conscious evolution supports you in becoming the clear, resonant vibration of your spiritual gift in your human form. This is a path to *presence*—to bringing the presence of Spirit, the deep divine within, into full form as you. As the energy of the core distortion is dissipated, and as you become increasingly clear and attuned to the energy field of your spiritual gift, the Genesis Pattern within you will be renewed. The shimmering light of your life force energy will flow freely as you stand in the center of yourself and all of creation. As you come to *be* your spiritual gift you become liberated from the entangled, burdensome energies, patterns, and habits of the core distortion, allowing ascension into a new stage of being—a new stage of consciousness along the unfolding pathway of your soul's infinite evolution.

As you walk your path with the knowledge of your gift, you can then explore questions such as:

- What does it mean to *be* this gift?
- What do I need to clear, release, and heal so that I can discern the next steps on the path of evolving this gift?
- How might this gift guide me?
- What are the teachings and the wisdom from others about this gift?
- What practices will help me deepen and evolve this gift?
- How might I fully integrate this gift in my life?
- How does this gift shape me as a vessel of life?
- What are ways that I might offer this gift to all of life?
- How might I offer this gift for the evolution of the world and the cosmos?

This is a conscious process of drawing your attention to the field of higher consciousness of your gift, and then using your intention to consciously evolve.

You are coming to be your gift, which is the process of bringing yourself—your divine self—into full *presence* in each present moment of this life. Your full presence here will impact the unfolding of your spiraling evolutionary path of coming to be the shimmering lights of creation in the form of a human *being*. As I have reflected upon my continuing evolutionary work and nudging myself—stretching—farther along the path, Rumi's words have inspired me:

You have drunk from this wine,
but there is still some left.
Go for another round,
the real stuff is in the last sip.[5]

Taking the last sip, bringing your presence into even fuller form, also creates new possibilities for awakening others. When your energy field fully vibrates to the energy of your spiritual gift, that vibration, through your presence, can awaken others to activate their own spiritual gifts and to evolve. The evolution of your spiritual gift becomes a gift for all of creation.

My Journey Through the Four Portals

My spiritual gift is *Peace*. Knowing my gift has been powerful, energizing, and uplifting. This knowing has helped me synthesize many aspects of my spiritual journey. As I reflect upon my life, I can see now that my path with *Peace* was present from the very beginning. It has been the fundamental focus of my life, and also my offering to others. As I continue my work with the first portal, I invoke *Peace* in many different ways throughout each day.

The energy of my core distortion has surfaced throughout my life as a sense that "I don't get it right." Someone else's may be that "they are undeserving," or that "they are not enough," or that "they are not completely lovable." Mine is about "not getting it right."

As was mentioned earlier, there are many layers of distortions that are woven together and feed each other. While in the course of working with dissipating the energy of my *core* distortion, I found a related distortion thread that has repeatedly surfaced as well. That thread is a sense of separation and fragmentation—of not being in a state of unity. The voice of the distortion told me, yet again, that this is a way that "I don't get it right"—I'm not in a state of unity.

"*I*"—the deep, divine being within—has always known that this was not true, but the energy of the core distortion was masking the truth. My conscious evolutionary work in the second portal has greatly dissipated these distorted energies. The jagged edges created by the core distortion have been reduced, and I have come to feel and know *Peace* in an entirely new way. I have remembered that I am already *Peace*. This frequency is embedded in my light matrix. It is my gift. Through this continuing evolutionary process, I am deepening my knowing of this gift of *Peace*, and it now vibrates more clearly within me.

My work in the third portal with the sacred spiraling breath has helped me create a clear pathway for this knowing and for the energy of *Peace* to move throughout me. And in the fourth portal, as I have engaged in fusing with the purity of the ground field of creation and restoring the Genesis Pattern within, I am more fully coming to *be* the gift of *Peace*. I continue to take this infinite journey of walking the pathway of conscious evolution—a path of light and creation. This has been a blessing for which I am deeply grateful. My hope is that your journey through the gateways of the four portals of the Rainbow Wheel map for conscious soul evolution will be blessed with the vision that Rumi describes when he writes:

The gates made of light
swing open. You see in.[6]

Many Ways to Journey

There are many ways to take this journey of conscious evolution using a wide range of tools, methods, and practices, some of which will be suggested in the next several chapters. Perhaps you will step through this portal process just as described. Alternatively, you might hold the intention of coming to be your spiritual gift and then find that a gateway for manifesting your intention simply opens as you live life. For many, some combination of these two ways will be a part of the journey.

The following imagined tale is based on my glimpses from the light of the whirling Rainbow Wheel. This is a fictional story offered as one illustration of how holding the intention of evolution can open portals for transformation. Envision a circle of friends that has gathered around a fire to listen to a fictional traveler's adventure. I invite you to join the circle to hear the words of how an evolutionary journey *might* unfold.

> *I was on an island in the wilderness, surrounded by huge old pine trees, shimmering lakes, eagles, loons, and an occasional lake otter. I experienced many changes of weather while on this journey, and at this particular moment the wind was feisty and gusty, and there were thundering clouds rolling my way from the west. The air felt charged and my heart was pounding. But I noticed that my breath was calm and that created some momentary balance within me. This had been a very reflective journey, which was my intent. I held some questions about my purpose in this lifetime that I hoped I would gain some insight about. I felt that this approaching storm might bring that insight.*
>
> *The storm felt like it was mirroring my inner tumultuous state of being. The world around me was altered from this storm. There was electricity in the air. The waves were hitting the rocks on the island, the trees sang as the wind blew, and the distant sound of thunder stirred every cell in my body. Everything was touched, charged, and moved.*
>
> *I climbed up to the top of a rock outcropping on the island to perch and watch and experience the approaching storm. There was a protected area lower down, underneath this outcropping, and so I planned to move there for protection from the elements once the storm was closer. The energy of storms has always called to me. It feels as though the sheer power of the storm rips away layers that have become stagnant. I called for the stagnating energy within me and surrounding me to be lifted and cleared so that I might flourish in a new way. I could feel the storm's energy growing, and as it did the yearning within me to be freed, to be released from an old, crippling energy that I felt and carried with me, also grew. In fact, as the*

storm neared, I could actually feel this crippling energy grow heavier and more present within me. I felt I was ready to burst.

    I sat quietly while the wind swirled around me. I was in a vortex of energy. I closed my eyes and went deeper and deeper into the center of that vortex, and as I reached the center I could feel a place of stillness and deep quiet. I focused on the pulse of my breath. I could also hear the quiet sound of my heart beating, like a rhythmic dream beat, and with each beat I had a sense of stepping or sinking down farther and farther, as if going into a cave. The external sound of the thunder added to the cacophony of sounds escorting me into the cave. After a while I began to feel as though my breath was one with the wind—the breath of the earth—and my heartbeat was one with the pulse of the earth. I could almost hear her turning on her axis, moving, pulsating, breathing. I could still hear the external sounds, but it was as if they were faint and very far away. It was an eerie sensation, and yet it felt completely right.

    In that deep quiet, I felt a sense of oneness, I felt the interconnectedness of all of the universe. Then, because of that knowing, I also became aware of a heaviness within me that I was holding in my midsection that didn't match the energy of the oneness. This was that crippling energy within me.

    Suddenly I knew that the crippling energy was the opposite of oneness. It was fragmentation and separateness. It was the feeling of never doing enough, knowing enough, or being enough that had plagued me my entire life, often in very subtle ways, but always present. I was always trying to find a way to be the everythingness of the one universe, the interconnected universe, the universe that was whole. And now with another flash of lightning I knew that I always am, always was, and always would be that wholeness, that oneness of the universe. I was experiencing that right now and knew this to be the truth. So, I gathered together all of that other crippling energy into a ball in the center of my body, and released it into the wind, the rain, and the lightning. The air, the water, the fire, and the earth that I was sitting upon would transform this energy for the good of the whole. This act would restore balance and integrity, establishing a new landing from which to continue my evolutionary work.

    I began to hear my breath again and the beat of my heart. Breath. I began to focus on my breath and on the breath of the earth, which I was experiencing this moment with the wind. I mentally knew that a meaning of the word "breath" has to do with "spirit," and now I was feeling it. I began to contemplate the connection between the breath of *life and spirit as I felt the breath of life swirling throughout my body. I knew that working with this connection of breath and spirit would lead me on the next part of my spiritual journey. It would be a key to unfolding and evolving my life's purpose. It would bring me into a new stage of being, of presence.*

As I sat in a deeper sense of oneness than I had ever before experienced, I had both clarity and wonder—clarity about the fundamental unity of creation, and wonder about how my life path would be affected by this knowing, about how I would bring this new sense of myself into all that I am and do. And while I wondered about what my path might look like, there was no doubt that it would be profoundly affected by this experience, because "I" was now here in a new way.

I offered my gratitude to all of the elements that had guided me to the insights and knowing of this journey, and then took shelter down below just as the winds intensified, and the rain began to fall.

Your Sacred Journey

The Rainbow Wheel map offers four portals for conscious soul evolution. While you may find the specific pathway provided by these portals useful, there are many ways in which these types of evolutionary experiences might occur. Although the fictional traveler's journey described in the preceding tale involved the work of invocation, liberation, breath, and renewal (the pathway of the four portals of the Rainbow Wheel), the way in which it unfolded was unique:

Portal One: *Invoking Your Spiritual Gift.* The traveler's gift of *Breath* was revealed as part of the experience of the journey, and this gift was acknowledged and invoked as the traveler called for the wind—the breath of the earth—to break apart stagnating energy.

Portal Two: *Liberating the Gatekeepers.* The traveler felt the crippling energy of the core distortion of *never knowing, doing, or being enough*. Energies of the core distortion were intentionally dissipated and released as a part of this journey.

Portal Three: *Spiraling Breath.* As the storm approached, the breath was whirled throughout the traveler's body, clearing a pathway for the energies of the gift, and again after releasing the stagnating energy.

Portal Four: *Renewing the Genesis Pattern.* Having dissipated and cleared some of the previous illusions and stagnating energy, the traveler, with a flash of lightning, fused with the pathway of knowing the unity of creation—the Genesis Pattern. The traveler also committed to bringing this new sense of "I"—*presence*—into full form, knowing there would be work to do in bringing this forth.

The portals of the Rainbow Wheel map suggest a pathway that you can follow for consciously evolving. However, the specific details of that path will be unique to you. The traveler in the preceding tale wasn't following a particular map. There was clear intention to evolve, and a specific question (*What is my life purpose?*) that was being explored. The traveler had a deep connection to the wilderness and actively chose that as the place for this experience.

So while the traveler didn't have a copy of the Rainbow Wheel map in hand, the underlying principles of the map—intention, choice, attention, an openness to being in the opportunities of the present moment, commitment to an evolutionary process, and practices to support and guide that process—were present and engaged. Whether you choose to move through the portals as suggested in the following pages, use the guiding ideas of the portals to create your own pathway, or some combination of these two ways, the Rainbow Wheel map offers support for the unfolding of your magnificent conscious soul evolution.

Practices for Conscious Soul Evolution

Integrating Practices—practices to support embracing, anchoring, and integrating the effects of conscious soul evolution.

•Preparing to Work with the Portals

The process of conscious evolution is built upon your choice to evolve your soul. Thus, the first step of this process is to *intend* to evolve. *Intending* directs your attention and aligns your energy field toward evolution. There are many different ways in which you might do this, and in fact it is very possible that you already have.

I suggest that as you begin your journey with the Rainbow Wheel you go through a process of *intending* even if you have already done so as part of other evolutionary or spiritual practices. I often find that in the process of clarifying and restating my intention, new insights surface about my path. This *intending* process is in the realm of visioning, of being a seer of "you." Here is what I *intend* about my evolution:

I intend to consciously evolve my soul for the benefit of all. I see myself—and all—as being pure, crystal-clear light containing all of the potentiality of creation. I offer my gratitude and the fruits of my evolution for the benefit of all.

This is like a mantra for me and I focus my attention on it daily. Its energy creates a container—a field—from which I live my life and create my evolution. In this process of *intending* I also consciously open myself to new possibilities, and to becoming aware of opportunities that are in alignment with my intention to evolve.

Following is a way in which you might *intend* in addition to other ways that you may already be using. This practice supports you in creating a space for you to connect more deeply with yourself:

Select a location in which you easily feel connected to any of the spiritual gifts—*Peace, Love, Joy, Grace, Unity,* etc. This place could be in your home, or yard (perhaps on a balcony if you live in an apartment), or some other location—a park, garden, woods, an active urban square, an art gallery, a barn, or a meditation center. Enter this space and connect with the field of higher consciousness that has drawn you there. Take a few deep, cleansing breaths and settle into the sense of this field of higher consciousness. Feel yourself bathed in its light and its essence.

Then, using whatever form of expression you prefer—writing, art, movement, singing, humming—begin to formulate and create your intention. Ask yourself: *What do I intend?* You may decide to ask yourself this question several times, and you may find that each time you reach another level of intention.

Once you have formulated what you intend, take a deep breath and then release the breath. Focus your attention on your connection with the field of higher consciousness and then state the intention that you just crafted aloud—quietly if need be, even a whisper will do.

Each day, state your intention to yourself and to all of creation. The process of repeating your intention will help you anchor—or ground—it within. You might also consider journaling for a few weeks regarding what you notice about yourself or your life as you welcome in this practice of *intending*. Over time, revisit this *intending* process, allowing your intention to shift and change as a reflection of your ever-evolving consciousness.

Your Spiritual Gift

Consciously working with your intention helps to prepare you for opening more fully to the energy of your spiritual gift. Next, as you identify your gift and begin to explore it, continue to connect with your *intention* as your base—your grounding—for your evolutionary work.

4

Identifying Your Spiritual Gift

*The Light of Creation, Beauty, Gratitude, Breath,
Ascension, Compassion, Unity, Harmony, Joy,
Coherence, Peace, Love, Grace*

I became *consciously* aware of my gift of *Peace* about twenty years ago as I sat in a quiet space in my home. Appreciating the fragrant flowers that filled the room helped me reach a place of inner stillness. As I asked to consciously know the gift I carry and bring forth into the world, I found myself taking an inner journey through an exquisite field of rainbow-colored flowers, on a bright, sun-filled day.

I came to rest in this field with a deep sense of peace. And then I remembered this knowing from my first journey to the portal of light. I had previously experienced this peace. I also remembered that people, across my lifetime, had often mentioned that they felt a sense of peace in our friendships or work together. And as I reconnected with experiences of peace I already encountered, I felt a vibration throughout all of my being—all of my hair was standing on end! I realized that I already had a deep knowing that my gift was *Peace*.

Your gift awaits you, and it is offering you an entryway to your soul's evolution. As you consciously acknowledge and work with your gift, you are weaving the shimmering fabric of life.

Your Gift

The spiritual gifts—the fields of higher consciousness—that are a part of the Rainbow Wheel have been a focus of humanity in many different forms throughout time. We have written poems, painted, sculpted, danced, and created symphonies, operas, and songs attempting to convey our deepest inner understandings of these fields. We have traveled the globe seeking the natural wonders of the earth in special places where we might experience these gifts in new ways. We've joined together in communities of many types to create and nurture relationships that might bring us new insights about these energies of higher consciousness. And yet, your spiraling journey with your spiritual gift, and its many stages of evolution, is uniquely yours.

The thirteen specific gifts identified as being a part of the Rainbow Wheel are offered as potential access points for soul evolution. They are strategic points for more deeply entering your spiral of evolution, and consciously directing your attention to any one of them (or their layers) can have a significant effect. One may look at the wheel of gifts and wonder: *What about other gifts? Is this the whole list?* These gifts each have many layers. They are multidimensional—there are gifts within gifts.

For example, you might identify your primary gift as "radiance," which in the Rainbow Wheel could be identified as a layer of the gift of *The Light of Creation*. Or your gift may be "generosity," a layer of *Gratitude*. There are many nested layers that comprise each gift. The list of these thirteen named gifts is absolutely *not* a complete list of all possible gifts of higher consciousness. It is, however, *a* list with great potential for contributing to soul evolution.

Paying attention to your primary gift is like having a key for opening and evolving all of the higher frequencies—*all* of the gifts—within you. The frequencies of all of the gifts strengthen and evolve from your work with your primary gift, or from your work with *any* of the gifts. However, since your primary gift has a slightly stronger vibration, it can readily offer you an entryway to the next stage of your evolution, making it a good place to start focusing your attention. And as noted in Chapter 3, at some point in your process you may begin to recognize other gifts that are vibrating with the same strength as your primary gift.

As the frequencies of the gifts strengthen and evolve, they also affect others simply through your presence here, and through your intentional offerings to the whole of creation. This is a gift on many levels. All of life is connected—interwoven into the fabric of creation, and we are all made of the same light and star stuff. We all resonate together. Therefore, as your frequency strengthens and evolves, it affects everyone.

So, what is *your* spiritual gift? While there are many different ways you might go about identifying your gift, the following guided meditation is provided to help you with this process. You may find this useful by itself, or perhaps in conjunction with other methods you have previously used for meditation and accessing deeper levels of yourself. Or you may already know what your gift is—perhaps you have had a sense of this for many years, or as you have read this book it might have just jumped out and made itself known. In that case, this meditation can be used to help you in *further* exploring your gift.

Directly following the meditation you'll find brief stories about key energy attributes for each gift. You can either go through the meditation first and then read the narrative about your gift as a support for more deeply working with it, or you might find it useful to read all of the stories first. Do whatever feels like the right approach for you in identifying your gift.

It is important to remember that there is no wrong answer! All of the gifts and their layers are energetically connected—they are inextricably interwoven and reflected within each other. So if you identify your gift as *Joy* and then at some point later in your life come to see that your primary gift is *Unity*, nothing will have been lost. Your work with one gift impacts all of them because they are all interconnected—they are all strands of a larger field of higher consciousness. Perhaps upon reflection you will find that you first needed to work with *Joy* in order to come to a place of knowing that you are the spiritual gift of *Unity*. All of the gifts are contained within your soul, and all will evolve with your conscious attention being placed on any one of them.

Also, you may have a sense of the vibratory strength of more than one of the spiritual gifts. ***If at the end of the following meditation you have come away identifying more than one gift, or if you simply are uncertain whether one vibration is slightly stronger, that's fine, too. The point here is to find a focal point for your evolutionary work at this moment.*** It's okay if your focal point involves two gifts, or even more. Since you have brought all of your prior evolutionary work with you into this lifetime, it is very possible that other spiritual gifts are already matching the vibrational intensity of your primary gift.

You may find, like some people that I've worked with, that you do not identify any one of the gifts as having a stronger vibration at this time. ***In that case, just choose one that resonates for you—that lights up or speaks to you—and begin your work there.***

Eventually, with this evolutionary process, you may notice that one gift naturally comes forward more frequently or more strongly, and identifies itself to you as *your gift*. Or you may hear other people speak about you in a way that resonates with one of the gifts, giving you a clue about a stronger vibration that others notice in you. Remember, the intention is to create soul evolution, and although there are definitely themes, ways, and practices that humanity has become aware of across the ages for creating evolution, there are also many entry points for doing so.

Guided Meditation for Identifying Your Gift

To connect with the fields of higher consciousness, some people use meditation, while others use ceremony, ritual, breathwork, chanting, guided meditations and visualizations, or dreamtime work. The following are a few preliminary reflections on a guided meditation—*The Clear Light of the Heart* meditation—that originated both from my work with the Rainbow Wheel and from learning about and experiencing different types of meditative forms. You can use it to connect with these higher fields in order to identify your spiritual gift. This meditation brings you to a realm outside of current time and space into the realm of higher consciousness and the ancient wisdom of creation that is present within the clear light of each of our hearts. The Resources section at the end of the book lists a few sources of other meditations that you may also find helpful for reaching this realm.

The Clear Light of the Heart meditation connects you with the guiding light of your heart. As you step into the beam of clear light in the heart, stay open to all possibilities. Although some people follow the meditation precisely, others begin the meditation and then find that their experience diverges from these written instructions. Some people are more visual and "see" every step as it is written. Others are more "auditory" and begin to have experiences that are based more in sound; still others may dance, fly, or spin their way into the wisdom of the clear light of the heart. Some have a more linear experience, as written here, and others engage in a "sense" of the experience. Allow this process to unfold in your own unique way.

In this meditation you will have the opportunity to identify your spiritual gift. Remember that the Rainbow Wheel gifts of *Peace, Love, Joy, Unity*, and so on have been offered as key strategic access points for soul evolution. There are many layers within each of these, however, so if another one comes to you as part of this meditation, go with it—let this process unfold in the way that is most meaningful for you. And, if you know your spiritual gift and feel no need to ask this question at this time, you can either skip over this part and read the rest of the chapter, or you can use this meditation to help you further explore your gift. For example, you can substitute the question in the meditation about identifying your gift with a question such as: *What wisdom about my gift would help me in this moment on my evolutionary path?*

Here are the instructions for *The Clear Light of the Heart* meditation (an audio file of this meditation is available at the author's website, www.joelise.com):

Begin by lying on your back or sitting in a comfortably supported position. Close your eyes and breathe deeply to clear yourself. Breathe in through your nose and release the breath out through your mouth, cleansing yourself of all tension being held at this moment. Breathe easily and deeply, filling yourself fully with your breath—filling your lungs and your abdominal area. As you release the breath, release any tension and stress you have been holding. Take a full breath in through your nose, and release the breath out through your mouth. And when you are ready, bring your breath to a gentle and rhythmic state, changing the breath pattern to gently inhaling through your nose, and also gently exhaling through your nose. Continue to feel your body filling with the breath, your belly and chest expanding and releasing with each cycle of the breath.

Now, put your right palm on your heart. Gently breathe into your heart. See the breath flow into all of the chambers of your heart, and as you breathe see that the breath is made of pure, clear light. Feel the light filling all of the chambers of your heart, and as it does so, see your heart opening like a beautiful flower coming into full bloom. Know that you are in the center of the clear light of creation. With each breath see the light filling every fiber of your physical body and your energetic field. Also see the light moving out beyond you, filling all of the space around you with this luminous, brilliant light of creation.

Offer your gratitude for the love of this light and then send the light above and below for the benefit of All. With the inbreath, fill all of yourself with the light. With the outbreath, see the light flowing out of you to all of creation. It is moving out the top of your head—your crown chakra—to the sky, and it is flowing out the bottoms of your feet to the earth. With each complete cycle of the breath, the light fills all of you and all of creation.

Now, focus your breath on the heart, breathing the light into your heart. As you bring your attention to this heart space, state your question: **What is my spiritual gift?** Now follow the light of your breath into your heart. See yourself taking a gentle walk on a pathway in the most beautiful place in all of the cosmos. Know that the light of this place will guide you. As you follow the light of your breath on this gently flowing path, you will arrive in a magnificent valley. You may be surrounded by the energy of the ancient wise trees, or rainbow gardens of light, or sacred pools of healing water, or sandy, windswept beaches. Open to receiving the beauty that surrounds you. Notice all of the life forms and take in the sounds and the fragrances.

As you reach the end of the pathway, continue moving to whatever area resonates for you, to wherever you are drawn—go wherever the light of your breath guides you. It may be similar to the pathway that brought you here, or it may be entirely different. Go to where the light of the breath leads you. You may continue walking on a path, or you may go through another opening or gateway. You may find that you move by walking or perhaps you will fly, or you might simply appear in another location. You may be in the chamber of a cave, in a pool of water, in an ocean, on a mountaintop, in a desert, or in a forest. Just follow the clear light of your breath.

You are in the center of the wisdom of the cosmos. You have stepped into a beam of cosmic light containing all—*all* of the energy and *all* of the wisdom of the cosmos. This is an ancient sacred space—an invocational field for accessing the higher realms of universal knowledge and wisdom. What is spoken, experienced, or known here is the truth of the heart. You may find the answers to your question about your spiritual gift with the help of a guiding energy that has a specific form, such as an animal guide, a human guide, or a guide of some other form. Or you may connect with a guiding energy that has no specific form. You may find that you simply "know" the answer to your question. The trees, the wind, the water, the air, the earth, or the light may inform you.

You may have an experience that is similar to taking a journey and you may find yourself transported to another place. Or, you may stay where you are. You may hear sounds or vibrations that communicate to you. You may sense or know things that relate to the answers to your question. Just let this unfold. You are in the center of the inner clear light of your heart, the center of all of creation. Now, ask your question: ***What is my spiritual gift? And then let your experience unfold.***

When your experience is complete, return to the pathway that brought you into the valley. Then, follow the light of your breath back up along the pathway, back up to where we first began our journey. When you are ready, bring yourself back to the present physical realm, the present time, the present place and open your eyes.

After completing *The Clear Light of the Heart* meditation, consider journaling about your experiences and the information you accessed. This may be words you received, visual images, or simply what you came away *knowing*. Journaling can be a powerful tool for focusing the information you've gained, and reflecting on what you've learned and where you think you need to go next in formulating your spiritual journey. Journaling may help you to bring a more ethereal experience into this realm of matter and form.

In *The Right to Write*, Julia Cameron says that writing connects us "both to our own insights and to a higher and deeper level of inner guidance as well ... Higher forces speak to us through writing. Call them inspiration, the Muses, Angels, God, Hunches, Intuition, Guidance, or simply a good story—whatever you call them, they connect us to something larger than ourselves."[1]

Author and writing instructor Christina Baldwin writes in *Storycatcher*, "I believe the kinds of writing millions of us are doing in our diaries and journals are attempts to heal the split in the human mind and in the human experience ... What we create through this kind of writing is neither art nor reality, it is something new: the story of our lives."[2] Journaling may help you deepen your understanding of the experiences you have in the space of *The Clear Light of the Heart* as you tell yourself this story of your life. Also, as you journal you may discover new questions that you would like to bring to this heart space. Remember, you can journey back to *The Clear Light of the Heart* with any of your evolutionary questions, at any time.

Energy Threads of the Gifts

The spiritual gifts of the Rainbow Wheel (*Love, Beauty, Grace*, etc.) have been experienced and spoken about in many ways across the ages. Although recurring themes appear, there are endless ways in which these themes can be carried within us, felt, and communicated about. We each may access different aspects and truths about a gift and come to different understandings. Your knowings and interpretations may be somewhat different from mine because of our unique life experiences and our current stages of evolution.

Focusing your attention on a core energy—what I refer to as "core energy threads"—for each of the gifts can enhance your accessing of your own inner "truths." As you consciously work with your spiritual gift, it is suggested that you focus on the core energy listed for your gift in the stories offered next, and in the list that follows the stories, and see what you experience. These threads are potential starting points for your deeper exploration, and for opening to new levels and dimensions of your evolution.

The following brief narratives provide examples of how these core energy threads might be experienced by different people, given their particular stage of evolution in the present moment. While fictional, these stories are based on a combination of my work with the Rainbow Wheel and information from my work with others on their spiritual gifts. Imagine that a circle of people has gathered together to speak their wisdom about their gifts in order to help each other understand the gifts, and to support each other in evolving. Imagine that these thirteen people have been asked two questions:

- What is your spiritual gift and how does it affect your life?
- What is a core energy thread that you experience with this gift?

Following are the imagined responses from thirteen fictional people. Since different insights will become visible for us about these spiritual gifts based on our stage of evolution, this is a continuously unfolding process. The key word that summarizes the core energy thread being described in each story appears in bold letters:

A story for the gift of *The Light of Creation*
My gift is *The Light of Creation* and its core energy for me is **stillness**. Even though I'm often on the move, I realize that I need to ground myself in a sense of stillness. Before I move, I gather myself in that stillness, connect with the energy of the light, and listen. Then, I come to know—to sense—the way in which to move. Now, that doesn't mean that every move I make is what I would call calculated, or that I never take action quickly, because I do. In fact, I'm very spontaneous, which I think is also part of the gift of light. However, when moving quickly I almost always attempt to find a way, even if momentary, to connect with the light of creation—the source light of all—and sense what is needed. I hope that grounding myself in **stillness** can also be a gift to others.

A story for the gift of *Beauty*
My gift is *Beauty* and its core energy for me is **transcendence**. For me to truly experience my own sense of beauty, I find that I must transcend personal, cultural, familial, and historical assumptions and beliefs because they can create interference with cultivating my own knowing. I must transcend my former me so that I can discover new levels of beauty. I am always seeking beauty (in other people, in nature, in art and music, in comedy, etc.), and I am often surprised by where I find it. I hope that I am also able to help others, through connecting with the energy of **transcendence**, to find their own inner beauty. This is an art—the art of continually polishing the edges so that we can see our beauty, just like polishing a gemstone.

A story for the gift of *Gratitude*
My gift is *Gratitude* and its core energy for me is **synthesis**. To bring myself to being in a state of gratitude I synthesize many levels of appreciation. I connect with many levels of energy and information, weaving it all together, and gratitude

is what emerges from this process for me. It is like an energy eruption! I burst forth, my heart wide-open, and want to sing a song of gratitude. I weave the threads of life into a bouquet of light with different fragrances, and when people come in contact with this bouquet they feel gratitude. **Synthesis** is an energy-weaving process that, for me, brings forth much gratitude.

A story for the gift of *Breath*

My gift is *Breath* and the core energy for me is **tranquility**. This gift, for me, is about the rhythm of the river of the life force energy within. There can be many different rhythms of life. However, I find that through accessing a wave of *tranquility* through my breath, I can better ride all of the variations and changes of life. In doing this, I believe that I am more of a full partner with life, friends, family, work, and with all of the twists and turns of living my life. Others experience me as someone who is fluid and flexible—seeing and sensing the fluidity of life. I seem to breathe and move in a way that embraces the many rhythms of life. Through this state of being I can offer others a sense of *tranquility* and perhaps they, too, will then more clearly find their rhythm and breath of life.

A story for the gift of *Ascension*

My gift is *Ascension* and its core energy for me is **clarity**. This gift affects my life in multiple ways. For example, when faced with making decisions or considering multiple alternatives, or even when coming to know new people or adjusting to a new environment, my tendency is to pause and wait until I can "see," with clarity, from a higher perspective. This is much like being a bird and looking down from my treetop perch. From this view I see, sense, and feel. It can take time and sometimes people get impatient with me, but other times people appreciate what I can see from that vantage point. I've had to learn to give myself the space and time I need to take and hold this perspective. Once I have, the actions to initiate seem to be clear and in alignment with my center. And I believe that I grow in this process of ascending to take a new view because, with clarity, I often see things that I otherwise would not have.

A story for the gift of *Compassion*

My gift is *Compassion* and the core energy for me is **transference**. Compassion can have an illuminating effect. Entering into a state of compassion can allow one to bring new light to a life situation, and create the possibility for healing energy and information to be transferred to a place where it is needed. Sometimes that illumination occurs through gentleness. Often that's what people associate with the word "compassion." Yet I find that compassion can also, at times, have a sharper edge. Sometimes the most compassionate thing to do is to say no to someone, or to tell a person something they don't particularly want to hear. The energy of **transference** is a way of offering information, energy, and support to others. And when I enter into a state of self-compassion, I can also offer this to myself for my own growth and evolution.

A story for the gift of *Unity*
My gift is *Unity* and its core energy for me is **merging**. As part of my gift I have a sense or knowing about the possibility of merging different energies, like waves coming together in one pool, forming one body of water. I see the distinctive parts and also the whole—how the parts and the whole are really the same. In my work, social, and family circles I'm often the one who brings people together—**merging** into a greater totality. I find that I am able to think, feel, and know the wholeness of situations, and yet appreciate each of the parts, the pieces. Through practicing this type of seeing I hope that I am growing my capacity to serve the greater good.

A story for the gift of *Harmony*
My gift is *Harmony* and its core energy for me is **opening**. The word "harmony" conveys the idea of resonance—different notes coming into harmony. My experience is that harmony is about opening fully so that the frequency of one's sound (our own inner sound) can be heard and felt. When I'm listening to music and it ends in a resonant chord that sustains for several seconds, I can feel my heart open and energy just seems to radiate out. Opening creates new possibilities for creating and living life. My intention is to help myself, and others, to open and hear the harmonic sound of our own inner choirs. Perhaps by each of us more fully **opening** to hearing and knowing our own inner sounds, we can better create harmonies together.

A story for the gift of *Joy*
My gift is *Joy* and its core energy for me is **infusing**. People often find my gift of Joy to be what they call contagious, as if I am infusing them with joy. I think the energy of my joy offers them my sense of the embrace of life. I think of joy as being similar to the feeling I have when I plant seeds in the ground in the spring. Seeds sparkle with potential, and the earth embraces them, **infusing** them with the nourishment needed to create life. That's what joy does to me: it embraces me

with the fullness of life. I'm delighted when people receive my joy because then I'm able to pass along the embrace.

A story for the gift of *Coherence*

My gift is *Coherence* and its core energy for me is **integrity**. When you call for assembling all of the pieces together—cohering—into a new integral form, you are creating. For me this gift is about a type of integrity that reveals or creates new insights. One of the ways my gift is used in life is that I can often help people bring different ideas and perspectives together in such a way that they can see new dimensions they couldn't see before. A shift of focus can create a new sense of the entire essence of the group, and a new understanding of its work or its purpose for being together might emerge. And individuals can have new insights into themselves. My experience is that this gift of *Coherence* and its energy of **integrity** can ignite higher knowing.

A story for the gift of *Peace*

My gift is *Peace* and its core energy for me is ***flow***. I consciously connect with what I refer to as the Great Oneness—the oneness of all of creation. This connection with the knowing of this wave of the oneness of creation establishes a flow of energy that brings me into a state of balance and supports my continuing growth and evolution. And when I am more fully living from this state, I can also better support others in finding their own flow and balance. Others have told me that they feel calmed by my presence. I think this calming sense is about the energy of ***flow***.

A story for the gift of *Love*

My gift is *Love* and the core energy for me is the energy of ***All***. It is about the fullness of life, about *everything* that is possible. Life is simply overflowing in every corner and from every crevice with possibility. I love the idea—the knowing—of the potentiality of all, and I bathe myself with the love of this knowing. I believe I take the actions of my life from this place. I know this might sound like I'm always enthusiastic, but I have my moments of discouragement right along with everybody else. Generally, though, I do launch each day from the state of loving ***All***. And I also begin my day by embracing the possibility that all of life for all beings everywhere will unfold from this place of Love.

A story for the gift of *Grace*
My gift is *Grace* and its core energy for me is the energy of the **center**. Grace keeps me standing right in the center of creation. When you are in the center you can look all around and see all of the energies of life, of creation swirling all around and within. In this state, I feel that I'm in the center of the interior of wholeness—the depths of the void of creation. To me that's the energy of *Grace*—knowing the wholeness of life from the center of creation, including all of the ways that life unfolds, both challenging and joyful. I feel a radiance and glow emanating as I stand in the **center**—as I stand in *Grace*. My hope is that as I attempt to live life from the center, I am able to offer that energy to others.

Vibrations for Evolving the Spiritual Gifts

We live in a world of frequencies. In *The Holographic Universe*, Michael Talbot summarizes the work of neurophysiologist Karl Pribram, saying that although Pribram began by studying the frequencies of sound and light, he eventually began to speak in broader terms about the "frequency domain." According to Talbot, Pribram "thinks that when mystics have transcendental experiences, what they are really doing is catching glimpses of the frequency domain."[3]

The gifts of the Rainbow Wheel are part of this domain of frequencies. The core energy threads discussed in the brief stories are also frequencies. So, too, are the colors that have been noted previously as having the potential to enhance your work of accessing your spiritual gift. Following is a summary of the spiritual gifts, a core energy thread that may support accessing the gift, and a color to visualize that can further assist in amplifying the resonance of this gift within you (more will be said about these color frequencies in Chapter 5).

Gift	Energy Thread	Color
The Light of Creation	Stillness	Golden
Beauty	Transcendence	Yellow
Gratitude	Synthesis	Green
Breath	Tranquility	Cobalt Blue
Ascension	Clarity	Indigo Blue
Compassion	Transference	Deep Purple
Unity	Merging	Violet/Lavender
Harmony	Opening	Red
Joy	Infusing	Magenta/Pink

Gift	Energy Thread	Color
Coherence	Integrity	Orange
Peace	Flow	Ultraviolet
Love	All	White
Grace	Center	Clear Light

Each of these—the gifts, core energy threads, and colors—are different types of frequencies in the frequency domain of the ground field of creation. This is just a possible starting place for your exploration. Trust *your* own knowing of the energy threads and colors that may help you amplify your work.

Many Ways to Identify Your Spiritual Gift

Throughout your life there any many different ways in which you can come to discover your spiritual gift, learn to consciously evolve it, offer it to others, and to come to *be* this gift. There are many ways to arrive at this knowing. You may have had a keen sense of your gift for much of your life, or perhaps you've had a general awareness—a hunch.

The Rainbow Wheel map provides a route you might follow in discovering your core spiritual gift. But there are many ways, other than this map, through which this knowing might occur. Stories, whether they are actual accountings or imagined tales (or perhaps a bit of both), can help us arrive at our own inner knowing. Come join me around the central hearth to hear an imagined tale that illustrates one of the many ways that knowledge of your spiritual gift can come to you. Perhaps, as with the fictional person in this story, you might ask for this information in dreamtime:

> *One beautiful spring day when I was in my early twenties, my grandmother came to see me. I was delighted and honored to have her visiting with me. My grandmother asked me to walk with her into a small wooded area where life soon would begin to grow. As we walked into the woods, Grandmother asked me to put my hands palms down on the ground, to feel the earth, and to listen. This was not an unusual request from my grandmother. She spent much of her time throughout the year tending to the plants and animals, finding stones and rocks that she arranged in various ways, or just sitting in the sun while quietly listening. She had always been a very gentle and reflective person.*
>
> *I bent down and placed my palms on the earth, which at first touch felt wet and cold. But after about a minute, my hands seemed*

to warm the earth beneath them and I could feel myself sink into her. Grandmother leaned over close to my ear and whispered, "The earth has a gift for you. She knows your heart. She knows your spirit. Listen to her and she will give you her gift. It is a gift of knowing something special about you. Listen." I listened with all of my heart and though I didn't hear words, I felt a wave of anticipation move throughout me. I noticed there was a stone buried in the earth beneath my hands. Grandmother instructed me to dig out the stone and hold it, and as I did so, she took a tiny piece of a dried plant from her pocket and placed it where the stone had been.

Then she took my hands and placed them in hers. As we stood, she told me that it was time for me to dream, and that when I lay down to sleep to ask the question, "What is my special gift?" Then she said I should just drift off to sleep, and that's what I did that evening. When I awoke in the morning I couldn't remember my dreams specifically; however, there was one word that I heard immediately and kept hearing throughout the day. The word was "love." I kept rolling that word around my head and feeling it in my heart. That evening Grandmother came to me and asked me to sit and tell her about my dreams. I shared that I couldn't remember the details of my dreams, but that when I awoke I heard the word "love." She smiled and told me that "love" is my gift. She explained that it is the gift given to me by Spirit, and the gift that I am given the opportunity to keep deepening and to offer to others. She said it is my path to experience this gift fully and to help others to know love within themselves. Grandmother said it is a gift about which I would gain much wisdom in my lifetime.

*I've spent my life journey exploring what it means to be the gift of love: What are the many dimensions of love? What is my responsibility? How does this gift guide me? What is the offering to others? What is the ancient wisdom of love? What are the teachings? How do I integrate this in all that I say and do? What does it mean to **be** Love? What needs to be released from me so that I am a clear vessel for being this spiritual gift of love?*

These questions have guided me since this experience with my grandmother, and this has been a blessing. I am so grateful for all of the gifts others have shared with me and it is my intention to offer the gift of love to help others in their unfoldment of life.

Your Sacred Journey

Having identified your spiritual gift or a gift that is drawing your attention at this time, the Rainbow Wheel process of consciously evolving now moves into the next stage—the first portal of the map of the Rainbow Wheel: Invoking your spiritual gift. But first, *Celebrate!* This is truly a joyous moment. You have consciously acknowledged your gift, or a gift that is calling to you in this moment, and so this is a celebratory time in your journey of coming to *be* your spiritual gift.

Practices for Conscious Soul Evolution: Celebrate!

Integrating Practices—practices to support embracing, anchoring, and integrating the effects of conscious soul evolution.

- **Celebrate!—Bask in the Glow of Your Gift**

Create a celebration to mark this moment of having acknowledged your spiritual gift, or a gift that is calling to you. This may be a quiet, internal celebration, or you might choose to include another person. You might take a walk in a place you enjoy, visit with a special friend, share a delightful meal, or take a day off from your "normal" daily tasks—a day of relaxation and renewal. Breathe in the full energy of your gift—bask in its glow. However you decide to do it, celebrate with intention—celebrate creation's gifts, and celebrate your deeper knowing of the divine within.

- **Celebrate!—Offer**

Reflect upon the ways you have been offering your gift to others (including people, plants, and animals) throughout your life. Reflect upon new ways that you might like to offer your gift, and then pick one and do it.

- **Celebrate!—Support Others in Identifying Their Gifts**

Consider gathering a small group of friends together to share your thinking about the spiritual gifts. You might even offer to take them through *The Clear Light of the Heart* meditation. Share with each other your experiences about your gifts.

Preparing for Portal One

Having identified your spiritual gift, or the field of higher consciousness to which you feel drawn, it is now time to step through the first portal of the Rainbow Wheel map for conscious soul evolution. In Portal One you invoke your spiritual gift—or any of the fields of higher consciousness—to support your evolution. As you prepare to participate in the practice of invocation allow Rumi's words to seep into your soul:

Open your hidden eyes and come,
Return to the root of the root of your own self. [4]

PART II

How Does the Rainbow Wheel Map for Conscious Soul Evolution Work?

o o o o o o o o o o o o o o o o o o o o o o o o o o o o o

The Rainbow Wheel map for conscious soul evolution offers a pathway for working with your spiritual gift to evolve your soul. Through invocation, liberation, breath, and renewal you evolve and create.

My heart is expanding a thousand fold.
                                                —Rumi

5

Portal One: Invoking Your Spiritual Gift

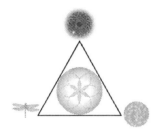

*You are in truth
the soul, of the soul, of the soul.*
—Rumi

Invocation intentionally summons forth a field of higher spiritual consciousness—a field in which you might more clearly know the *truth* of you as "*the soul, of the soul, of the soul.*" Ceremonies and rituals have been used since antiquity by the world's spiritual traditions to create invocational fields for the purpose of evolutionary work. These invocational ceremonies call us into a deeper space, connect us with higher consciousness, and awaken us to the limitless nature of life. They help us to unfold new possibilities from the ground field—the void, the plenum—of the cosmos.

When you step into invocational space and call forth the energies of higher consciousness, you are immersing yourself in that radiance. By invoking the vibrations of these higher fields, you are shining a light on that energy for your consciousness to look at, explore, and align with. You are, in effect, announcing your intention to *be* the energy of that field. And in the case of invoking your spiritual gift, you are announcing your intention to *be your gift*, in all of its fullness.

My own encounter with invocational fields began in the Jewish ceremonies of my youth. I have also come to experience and practice the invocational ceremonies of others—walking labyrinths, participating in Hindu puja ceremonies, learning to create the sacred space of the Medicine Wheel, and sitting in meditation. And ceremonies have also naturally arisen from within me as well—such as when I've taken myself to the sanctuary of the deep forest where I connect in my own way. There are many paths for invocation and bringing ourselves into a deeper connection with the divine.

In *Seven Whispers: Listening to the Voice of Spirit,* Christina Baldwin writes, "I have believed all my life that there is a necessary interaction that occurs between a person and the Divine. This interaction does not come only to prophets, bodhisattvas, and other great spiritual masters, it comes also to us: ordinary people in our ordinary lives. It is part of our natural human capacity to call out one of the thousand names of 'God.' And it is part of our human capacity to perceive and interpret the response."[1] Invocation initiates and engages such interaction between the person and the divine. It is a call to the divine—to a divine field of higher consciousness—and a way of opening to receiving the light of the response.

Invocational fields are energetic fields much in the way that gravity is a field. Just as gravity attracts and holds, so too do other types of energy fields attract and hold. In this case, invocational fields attract and hold a very high state of consciousness. Some, such as labyrinth pathways and stone medicine wheels, have been created by people, while others are naturally occurring and energetically embedded into the form of the Earth, sometimes being referred to as energy "vortices."

Over time, people have often constructed labyrinths, medicine wheels, and other sacred spaces in locations where they've experienced such naturally occurring energy vortices, thereby combining the earth's natural forces with consciously, human-made invocational fields. Some well-known examples are the circular ring of megaliths at Stonehenge, the temples at Machu Picchu, the Great Pyramid, Chartres Cathedral, and the kivas of Chaco Canyon. Both intentionally created and naturally occurring fields provide access points for attaining a high state of consciousness—places for coming into clearer alignment with these vibrations. Whether it is labyrinths, medicine wheels, domed sanctuaries, or pyramided steeples reaching for the divine, we are drawn to create containers to consciously connect with creation's highest energies.

The human body also contains such vortices, often referred to as "chakras," a Sanskrit word meaning "wheels of light." The chakras are vortices of energy that are always moving, always spiraling, with the light of these wheels emanating energy out and receiving it in. The chakra vortices are access points for connecting to invocational fields on earth and throughout the cosmos. As you step into invocational fields, the light and energy of divine spirit swirl into all of the fibers of your being through these whirling access points. You also offer this energy of higher consciousness to all of the cosmos through these chakras, in this amazing dance of life.

The Practice of Invoking Your Spiritual Gift

Invoking a field of higher consciousness requires *intention*: this is key to summoning forth the energy frequency of your gift or the field of higher consciousness you are calling to work with at this time. Intention acts like a beam of light, illuminating this frequency, and pointing your entire energy field in its direction. This beam of light connects you to the larger cosmic field of this gift. The process can be visualized using the infinity symbol, seen in Figure 8.

Figure 8.
Infinity Symbol

In this symbol there are two separate yet connected loops. One cannot be created and exist without the other. Just as with the infinity symbol, the process of invoking your spiritual gift has two loops. One loop is the field that you create with your intention to *be* the gift. The other loop is the field of that gift that exists as a part of creation as a whole. These two loops, or fields, are inextricably bound together. They create each other. One exists because of the other, and it is not possible to separate the two loops. Rumi describes this relationship when he writes:

The drop becomes the ocean
But the ocean also becomes the drop.[2]

By intending to be your spiritual gift, or any of the spiritual gifts, you assume the energetic wave—the signature—of that field of higher consciousness. By aligning yourself through your intention you attract the cosmic field of that frequency to you, thereby amplifying that energy wave within you. This is the process of invocation and evocation described in Chapter 3.

As you continue this practice on a regular basis, the amplification continues to grow and increase, and over time, more of your energy field has the resonance of this quality, such that *the drop* (you) *becomes the ocean*. And through the interconnection of the two loops, your intentional invocation has an impact on the whole of creation—*the ocean* (the cosmic field) *becomes the drop*.

This process is similar to what happens as a result of continually entering a state of meditation. Allan Combs suggests in *The Radiance of Being* that yogis repeating mantras in meditation are participating in a process whereby the mantra is "gently nudging the consciousness of the meditator"[3] toward subtle states of consciousness. And philosopher and author Ken Wilber reminds us that the more you are "dunked" into altered or meditative states, the more quickly you will move through a *stage*. He says that the state into which you are being dunked "acts as a *micro-transformative event*, disidentifying you from your present stage and helping you move to another."[4]

This effect of nudging and dunking is also the hoped for consequence of repeatedly and intentionally invoking your spiritual gift—creating a "micro-transformative event" that nudges you into being the field of your spiritual gift. One might refer to the invocational process as a means for attaining and aligning with *cosmic consciousness*. Psychologist Ralph Metzner, in *The Unfolding Self*, describes such alignment as an experience in which "the individual Spirit realizes its identity with the macrocosmic Creator Spirit ... awareness shifts from the separated individual to the unified cosmic perspective: the objects of the outer world, including planets, stars, and galaxies, are then seen to be within one's field of consciousness. At this point, then, the sense of self, the sense of who 'I' am, has also shifted. I am no longer just a separate human individual."[5]

Rather, the "I" is then known as being unified with divine consciousness. The process of invoking the field of your spiritual gift connects you to this field of cosmic consciousness, aligning you with all of its higher energies. Many cultures have described this process, with one such description coming from the Mayans. Working with Mayan information, researcher and author José Argüelles says, "If we were to give a modern name to this process ... it would be the principle of harmonic resonance."[6] He describes the Mayan view of a circuit of pulsing energy with a common origin and endpoint, like the infinity symbol illustrated in Figure 8. With harmonic resonance, the two loops begin to vibrate together as if they are one—the cosmic and the individual resonate as one.

Psychologist Jean Houston says "we are connected through what [biologist, Rupert] Sheldrake calls 'morphogenetic fields'—organizing templates that weave through time and space and hold the patterns for all structures, but which can be altered according to our changing thoughts and actions. Thus the more an event, skills, or pattern of behavior occurs, the more powerful its morphogenetic field becomes."[7]

Therefore, as you continue to invoke the field of your spiritual gift, that morphogenetic field that weaves across the realms of the cosmos will grow stronger. As the strength of the field of your gift grows within you, its effects will be felt everywhere through the whole of the morphogenetic field. Your personal and individual invocation, like the pebble in the pond, has an impact on the greater collective.

The results of researcher Masaru Emoto's studies on the effect of information on the shape of water crystals, provide a concrete example. You may be familiar with his work through the movie *What The bleep Do We Know?* Dr. Emoto photographs water crystals that have been exposed to words such as peace, love, and gratitude. As the water is exposed to these words (spoken or written), the crystals begin to change form, taking on beautiful shapes with an amazing clarity of light.

Emoto has repeatedly sampled water crystals coming from many different sources of both "clean" and "polluted" water, and has watched those crystals transform when exposed to words representing fields of higher consciousness. In *The True Power of Water*, Emoto asserts that "the quality of water changes based on the information it receives."[8] Just as with the water crystals, as you begin to consciously focus attention on the energy and light of *Peace, Love, Gratitude* or any of the spiritual gifts, your energetic field will change and the clarity of your light will increase.

I'd like to pause here for a moment to note that I am speaking about vibrations, resonance, and fields based on my knowing from what some would refer to as my "mystical" or "direct" experiences, not from "scientific" information. I believe this is an important distinction. While there may, at this time, be apparent similarities between the two areas of mysticism and contemporary science, whether or not there are actual convergences between these pathways is still unfolding. Quantum physicists are researching, theorizing, and discovering "new" ways of understanding how the cosmos works, scientifically speaking. This is a very different science from the one that most of us were reared with and educated about in our elementary and secondary schools. Quantum physicists themselves have been known to refer to this science as "bizarre."

While my own understanding of these scientific theories is infinitesimal, as I read books intended for the lay audience I am intrigued with how the new scientists and the ancient mystics at times *do* seem to be similarly hinting at the deep workings of the cosmos. Consciousness researcher Allan Combs writes in *The Radiance of Being* that we are walking "the razor's edge between science and mystery, but it is a path well worth treading. In our era, for the first time since that of the ancients, there is enough of a convergence between science and traditional wisdom to open an honorable dialogue."[9]

My own encounters with what I experience as the divine field of the light of creation beckon me to keep learning more about both the discoveries of the ancient mystics *and* today's quantum scientists. The ways in which these two areas might intersect will be fascinating, and I think, very important to pay attention to in the coming years.

There are many ways to "intend" and create this harmonic resonance that I have been speaking about in regard to invocation. But first it is important to recognize that at some level you are already doing this all of the time because it is your divine nature to *be* your spiritual gift. The process of *consciously intending* to be your gift allows you to deepen, ripen, and evolve this gift, thereby creating momentum for your soul's evolution.

Much of this invocational process at first bypasses the analytical mind, instead flowing through the circuitry of the heart mind—your heart knowing. The analytical mind becomes engaged eventually as it begins its process of attempting to understand the insights from the heart mind, the "ah-ha"s of heart knowing. This is part of the process of unfolding. You may find that the habits of your analytical mind leap forward to engage in and take over this process. But this is a process that begins in the heart, so still the mind and allow your heart knowing to first unfold. Gently speak these words of Rumi to the mind, as you step into your invocational field:

Shh. No more words.
Hear only the voice within.[10]

Ways of Invoking

There are many ways to invoke the field of your spiritual gift or any of the fields of higher consciousness. Two ways that you may find helpful for creating such invocational fields are sitting meditation and walking the labyrinth. These practices invite you into a nonordinary, higher state of consciousness that envelops you in the vibration of the higher fields of consciousness. These invocational forms can create a vortex of shimmering, luminous light that offers a way of moving into unity with all knowing, all wisdom of the cosmos here in your physical form. They provide a way of whirling into a state of harmonic balance with the oneness of creation.

In fact, whirling (a form of twirling around and around) is itself an ancient moving meditation and centering practice. Its intention is similar to that of labyrinth and sitting meditation practices—bringing you into your center and the oneness of all of creation. Shahram Shiva, a translator of Rumi's poems, many of which resulted from Rumi's own whirling practice, speaks about whirling as a way of creating an axis within our bodies: "Just as the Earth turns around its axis, or the entire solar system orbits around the Sun, or a tornado spins around its eye, or the electrons circle around the protons, we can create an axis within our body to whirl around it."[11] Through whirling around this axis, Shiva says that Dervishes (a term used to refer to some of those who practice this ancient whirling form) believe that "while they are whirling they are closest to the divine."[12]

While many forms of invocation originate from a variety of traditions, what is most important is finding a way that supports *you* in attuning to the fields of higher consciousness. The ancient sacred forms of invocation offer a depth and richness of experience. Learning about one or more of these forms can greatly facilitate and enhance your invocational experience. And it is also possible to simply and intentionally create a sacred invocational field by using a circle of flowers, candles, or stones that you step into with clear intention to create an invocational field. Taking a walk in the woods and standing beneath the trees, while grounding yourself with the earth and simultaneously uplifting your essence through the top of the canopy of trees, is another of the many ways to focus your intention and invoke a field of higher consciousness. Connecting with the rhythm of the ocean or a waterfall can help you to center yourself and align with your gift. Breathwork can also create an invocational field, and you will find that breathwork is usually an important part of most invocational practices.

Your Invocational Field Is a Blessing Chamber

Enter your invocational field and call forth your spiritual gift—or any of the gifts of higher consciousness—with both your silent intention *and* your words. Summon this energy of higher consciousness to you, and see yourself enveloped in its radiance; literally breathe it into every fiber of your being. And give voice to what you are calling forth:

> *the field of your spiritual gift (or the gift you are working with in this moment) filling every fiber of your being, resonating throughout, fully present with every breath*

Each time I enter the invocational field what I specifically say may vary. However, with focused, conscious, intention I often do say, "I invoke *Peace*." There are also times when silence and the intention in my heart create the invocational field without words.

Your Blessing Chamber is a field from which you can move along your spiraling path of stages of *being* your spiritual gift. At each new stage you will come to know your gift in a different way, and will interpret this journey of life using a new set of lenses. Creating an invocational field for conscious evolution is a blessing. The shimmering light of creation fills you with the fields of higher consciousness—your invocation creates a chamber of luminous rainbow lights. When you create an invocational field you are calling yourself to a chamber of pure intention to evolve soul and to offer the fruits of your evolution for all of creation. You are summoning forth evolution, as you stand in the brilliant light of your Blessing Chamber, glimpsing creation's possibilities.

Select the invocational form with which you will begin and choose a special place that has an uplifting and clear feeling for your invocational work. You may come back to this special place on a regular basis, or you may simply envision it from wherever you are continuing your invocational work.

You might also step into your Blessing Chamber before entering the dreamtime space. This is a way of moving into dream consciousness with pure intention and in resonance with a higher field. Then pay attention to your dreams, as you may find yourself experiencing this dreamtime state in a new way, accessing new levels of wisdom and knowing.

Following is a very brief description of meditation, and also the labyrinth, since you might find these two forms to be particularly accessible places for beginning the work of your Blessing Chamber. They are but two of the many sacred practices that you might use. There are many books, workshops, and guided experiences available about these, and other forms, some of which are noted in the Resources section at the end of this book. For example, if you are drawn to create a circle of stones for your Blessing Chamber, you may also be interested in exploring some of the listed resources to learn about the sacred way of the Medicine Wheel, which can incorporate a circle of stones.

What follows are just glances at how meditation and walking the labyrinth can be worked with to create a field for invoking your spiritual gift for the purposes of your conscious soul evolution. ***I strongly urge you to find out more about these and other forms that call to you.*** After the brief descriptions of these two forms there is a visualization that you might also find useful. It is based on my work with the Rainbow Wheel and can help you to begin your practice of invoking your spiritual gift and the radiance of its light.

Meditation

Since ancient times people have brought themselves into a deep inner state of openness, reflection, and contemplation. Meditation practices exist throughout the world. Some help bring the meditator into a deep state by focusing on mandalas, or meditation symbols such as the ancient Sri Yantra symbol (the name means "great object") shown here. Meditators breathe deeply and focus their attention on each triangle of the Sri Yantra, either moving from inner to outer and back again, or the reverse.

If you are interested in meditating upon the Sri Yantra, I suggest locating a copy—either printed or on the Internet—of the full-color image. The website www.chopra.com (in the "Meditation" section under "Chopra Center Programs") provides a color image along with a brief description of how to begin to meditate with the Sri Yantra. Other meditation forms might use mantras, chants, candles, bells, or flowers to help guide the way into a deeper state of consciousness. Many incorporate breathwork.

Meditation stills your mind, focuses your energies, and helps you to connect with your deeper self and become mindful of all that is present. Lama Surya Das, in *Awakening The Buddha Within,* describes the ultimate simplicity of meditation: "Meditation requires so little. All you have to do is stop doing whatever else you are doing, and just be there. You must be present to win. Just show up! Once you are accustomed to meditating, you can do it while standing, walking, lying, or even arranging flowers. The Buddha once said that there are four positions for meditation: standing, sitting, walking, and lying down. In other words, all the time."[13]

Surya Das teaches that through meditation we "can enter directly into more intimate, immediate engagement with our experiences in a way that reflects simplicity and a deeper, more authentic connection to life. This is not just about being more consciously alive. It's about *being* itself."[14]

Entering a meditative field can take a brief few moments or a longer amount of time. What is important is the quality of the meditator's intention and attention. Surya Das does many "one-minute meditations," and he says that doing so can keep awareness "fresh and vivid." Thus, with practice, you can quickly enter a focused meditative field and deeply invoke the field of your spiritual gift, or any of the gifts, calling that energy to you.

There are many volumes of works on meditation, some of which are simple and can be done by anybody rather quickly; others are more complex and can take years to reach the desired states. While there is a great variety, there are general guidelines that apply to most meditations, such as the ones Surya Das provides in *Awakening the Buddha Within*. As he reminds us, we can all do breath meditation, because "We are already breathing."[15]

The instructions for breath meditation simply help us to become aware of what we are already naturally doing, while also gently guiding us to focus and connect more deeply with higher consciousness. And while you are in this meditation field, if you choose to also summon forth any or all of the fields of the spiritual gifts, then that is the energy with which you will become saturated as you meditate.

The Labyrinth

The labyrinth is a pathway of silence, a sanctuary of breath and light. The breath of the silent walk brings you to the core of the center, filling you with the light of creation. Labyrinths are found throughout the world, and although they appear in different locations in various specific formations, they are always constructed as a circle with spiral paths leading to the center and back to the edge of the circle again. The image included here is the pattern of the labyrinth at Chartres Cathedral in France.

Labyrinths are based on the circle—which represents wholeness, unity, and the continuity of all life—joined with the spiral, a symbol for the eternal. With its spiraling pathway to the center of the circle, the labyrinth invokes the fullness of creation. Many communities around the world have created labyrinths that are open to the public, and an Internet search for your geographic area may help you to locate local resources.

The rhythmic flow and movement of this pathway, of this walk, *create* the invocation. This gentle whirling path connects and weaves the energy fibers of the universe within you, and attunes your consciousness to that of the unity of the cosmos. As this occurs, streams of light filled with the knowledge and wisdom of this unity merge within you. As you walk the labyrinth you are invoking the higher fields of consciousness and establishing harmonic resonance with these fields. Labyrinth guide Lauren Artress, in the foreword to Jill Geoffion's book *Praying the Labyrinth*, describes the labyrinth as "a path of prayer, a walking meditation that can become a mirror of the soul … The path becomes a metaphor for our own spiritual journey."[16] Geoffrion says that the labyrinth is "a pattern, an emblem, a walkway."[17]

By walking the labyrinth and entering into this whirling field, you become a focal point for the energies of the fields of higher consciousness, and the field of your gift. As you enter this powerful, silent, whirling invocational form, you might invoke your spiritual gift, or any of the gifts, and then walk in silence through its luminous light. Although this is a spiraling process with many layers and its own timing for each individual, working in an invocational field such as the labyrinth is central to the sacred path of conscious soul evolution.

With each turn of the spiral you are moving to your center, and the center of this whirling invocational vortex. Rumi's words provide guidance for this walk:

Let silence take you to the core of life.[18]

The Rainbow Wheel Spirals of Light

The Rainbow Wheel icon is a whirling wheel of light, a vortex of spiral energy that you can visualize and step into as an invocational field. Through invoking any of these gifts of higher consciousness you summon forth a specific energy vibration, and in effect, bathe in it. When you do this over time, you align your chakras and the whole of your energy field to this higher vibration. You align in stages as you immerse yourself in the field of your gift (or any of the gifts) and enact the practices of your evolutionary work. You move through spiraling stages of vibrating to and knowing this field as you literally become the vibration of your gift in form, manifesting higher spiritual consciousness in this earth realm.

Just as meditation or the sound vibration of a mantra can be used to "nudge" consciousness to this higher realm, so too can the vibration of color be used in this way. The colors suggested here for each of the spiritual gifts can support you in activating, accessing, and evolving these gifts. Filling your energy field with certain color tonations can help you to attune your field to the energies of particular gifts.

You may also feel called to visualize and summon colors other than those suggested here for your specific spiritual gift. There is no one color vibration that will always be what is needed for deepening the invocation of a particular spiritual gift. However, you may find it useful to *begin* by visualizing and calling forth the color vibrations suggested here:

> *The Light of Creation*—Golden
> *Beauty*—Yellow
> *Gratitude*—Green
> *Breath*—Cobalt Blue
> *Ascension*—Indigo Blue
> *Compassion*—Deep Purple
> *Unity*—Violet/Lavender
> *Harmony*—Red
> *Joy*—Magenta/Pink
> *Coherence*—Orange
> *Peace*—Ultraviolet
> *Love*—White
> *Grace*—Clear Light

Colors specified for three of the gifts require some special explanation. First, the color tonation of white for the gift of *Love* is not represented in the rainbow wheel image illustrated on the front cover of this book. The image is based on the rainbow, and since white is a reflection of all of the colors of the full spectrum of the rainbow, it does not appear separately in this image.

Second, the color tonation of clear light for the gift of *Grace* is not portrayed, again because the full spectrum of the rainbow does not include "clear light." Visualizing the clear light of crystal glass, for some, is a way of "seeing" this tonation and summoning it forth for evolutionary work. You might "see" that all of the color tonations come from the clear light, just as when you see a rainbow form in crystal-clear glass or crystal rock formations.

The third color tonation that is associated with one of the gifts, but that is not visually represented in the Rainbow Wheel image, is ultraviolet for the gift of *Peace*. Ultraviolet light has shorter wavelengths than is visible to the human eye. The ultraviolet radiations are beyond the color tonation of violet, which has the shortest wavelength that we can see.

Ultraviolet is specified as a color tonation that can assist in this evolutionary process even though you don't "see" it, because there is a frequency that still can affect your field. All colors are wavelengths of light, and it is the energetic vibration of the light that is affecting your field. The wavelength for the color we see as red affects your energetic field in one way, and the wavelength for the color we see as green affects your field in another way. This is the case with ultraviolet as well. Even though we cannot "see" the wavelength of ultraviolet with our eyes, our energy field is affected, just as our skin feels the effects of receiving ultraviolet radiation when we have a sunburn. When immersing yourself in the energy of ultraviolet for your work with the gift of *Peace*, use your higher vision to "see" beyond the color violet—reach beyond violet—and feel that radiation being absorbed by your energy field.

Please note that the color tonations suggested here for the Rainbow Wheel are not necessarily the same as other systems you may have encountered related to color therapy or chakra tonation. The colors here are specific to supporting your conscious evolutionary process of the Rainbow Wheel. While specific color tonations are suggested, you may sense different colors that would additionally help you with your invocational work. The auric field around the human body is an energy manager and will use all of the colors as they are needed to support your evolutionary work.

If you have not identified one of these specific gifts as being your gift, my suggestion is that you visualize yourself standing in the center of the whirling Rainbow Wheel icon and connect with whatever bright, luminous color is calling to you in this moment. Once again, bathing in any one or all of the vibrant, brilliant, rainbow-colored lights will assist you in this evolutionary process. To bathe in color vibrations to support your evolutionary work:

> *Visualize yourself as standing or sitting in the center of this whirling rainbow icon, and see yourself being bathed in whatever brilliant and luminous color radiation(s) you choose or are called to. Feel the color radiation(s) swirl throughout your entire body and energy field. Breathe the intensity of the color(s) into you. Absorb the energy of the shimmering rainbow light(s).*

You can also summon these vibrant colors to you when you are in meditation, walking the labyrinth, or sitting in a circle of flowers or stones. A color bath can enhance any of the invocational forms.

A Blissful Story About Invocation

Your experience in your Blessing Chamber—your invocational field—will be uniquely yours. Once again, I invite you to listen to an imagined tale about a fictional character that illustrates how a person's invocational pathway might unfold:

> *I am a whirling woman. That's how I've always seen myself. It all started when I was quite young. I whirled often. I loved the swirling colors swishing by me. And the feel of the air on the skin of my face, arms, and legs. I'd start out slowly spinning and then gradually pick up speed until the momentum of my own body seemed to just twirl me into other worlds. Eventually I'd just fall into a blissful heap on the ground. I began to notice patterns of experiences that would occur from my spinning around and around. There were feelings, sensations, and colors that would last for days. The colors were always luminous and the feelings were intense—intense joy and love. I would feel blissful when I was done, and it would stay with me for quite some time. My whole body would vibrate with bliss.*
>
> *As I grew, my whirling started to take on different forms: dancing, walking labyrinths, painting and drawing whirling forms, and silently watching and merging with the water of swirling creeks, streams, and rivers. What I've found is that all of these forms, for me, evoke a sense of the depths of possibility of creation. This energy wave of higher consciousness seems to be evoked from deep within me, and it also invokes the same energy wave from the whole of the cosmos.*
>
> *Here's an example of what I mean. I often take long walks that at some point involve connecting with moving, swirling water. I'll sit and watch the water, and at some point I just seem to merge into the cells of the water and feel the state of bliss that whirling always brings forth. It rises up from the center of my heart and then spreads throughout all of me. At the same time, I have a sense of a beam of light coming from above and filling me up as well. It starts as a luminous, vibrant, bright, white color and then also brings forth a golden hue. I see it as a column of light that radiates out from some distant point in the universe. It washes over me and then trickles down through the top of my head and fills all of me—every fiber of my being—with both*

white and golden light. It feels like the light contains all of the knowing of creation. It's a general sense of knowing with, at times, specific insights. Everything exists in this blissful light; all colors, all sounds, all forms—all knowing.

When I have these experiences, I truly know that there is no room for anything other than bliss within my being. Of course, I'm aware of and have a full range of other emotions and thoughts. And yet, I'm always able to come back to the grounding of this invocational field and the light of creation, its bliss and its many insights helping to guide me on my path.

Your Sacred Journey

May Rumi's words joyfully accompany you as you step into your Blessing Chamber to *Invoke Your Spiritual Gift*:

Fill me with the wine of your silence,
Let it soak my every pore
For the inner splendor it reveals
Is a blessing
Is a blessing.[19]

Practices for Conscious Soul Evolution: Invoking Your Spiritual Gift

Integrating Practices—practices to support embracing, anchoring, and integrating the effects of conscious soul evolution.

• Invoke Your Spiritual Gift

Continue to invoke your spiritual gift, or any of the fields of higher consciousness. Make this a daily practice. And at times throughout your day if you sense that you are not in alignment with this energy field, stop for a moment and invoke it. Using Surya Das's notion of the "one-minute meditation," quietly pause and take a breath, and in your inner eye bring yourself into your Blessing Chamber. Then invoke the field of your spiritual gift, or the gift you are working with at this time, and infuse yourself with its radiance.

- **Journaling**

Write about your experiences with your spiritual gift or any of the gifts, over your lifetime and in the present moment. You might journal about some of the following questions:

- What does it mean to *be* this gift?
- What do I need to clear, release, and heal so that I can discern the next steps on the path of evolving this gift?
- How might this gift guide me?
- What are the teachings and the wisdom from others about this gift?
- What practices will help me to deepen and evolve this gift?
- How do I fully integrate this gift in my life?
- How does this gift shape me as a vessel of life?
- How might I offer this gift for the evolution of the world and the cosmos?

General references about journaling practices are provided in the Resources section at the end of the book.

- **Art**

Engage in art practices that help you to explore your spiritual gift or the gift you are working with: drawing, painting, creating a collage, beading, making or coloring a mandala, composing a song, drumming the rhythm of this gift, sculpting, dancing, and so on. References for sacred art practices are provided in the Resources section.

- **The Clear Light of the Heart Meditation**

Journey to the clear light of your heart to explore and experience more of your wisdom about this gift. You can use *The Clear Light of the Heart* meditation, provided in Chapter 4, to gain further insight into your path with this gift. You might ask questions suggested in the following section (*Inquiry Practices*), or simply journey to the clear light of the heart and let your experience unfold.

Inquiry Practices—Individual Reflection and Exploration

A core purpose of a practice of inquiry is to free yourself from assumptions and beliefs (the *shoulds and shouldn'ts*) so that you can explore new possibilities and open new gateways for your unfolding evolution. (William Isaacs in *Dialogue and the Art of Thinking Together* provides information for enhancing your understanding of the role of assumptions in the practice of inquiry; see the Resources section.) Create a quiet space to reflect and explore the following, or other questions, about your spiritual gift. You might go for a walk in a place of beauty, or journal or engage in art practices while holding your questions. You might consider doing some breathwork to relax and enter a meditative state, travel to the clear light of your heart to explore your questions, or walk a labyrinth bringing your questions into that space with you.

- **Reflect and Explore**

Ask yourself questions such as the following. Really *live* these questions and see what emerges:

- In what ways am I currently embodying this spiritual gift?
- What do I need to know and learn about this spiritual gift to help me evolve?
- What are my assumptions (the *shoulds and shouldn'ts*) about this spiritual gift? If I suspend those assumptions what else arises? What is possible?
- What has been a major insight for me about this spiritual gift?
- What is forming, emerging, taking shape within my center as I evolve this spiritual gift?
- What questions do I notice are emerging for my contemplation about this spiritual gift?
- What actions might I take to allow me to further offer this spiritual gift to others, the world, and all of creation?
- What might be some of my next steps?

Sacred Circles—Collectively Reflect and Explore

When we reflect and think together, we tap into the collective wisdom of a circle of others joining us on this journey of conscious evolution. Moving from individual to group reflection encourages us to consider possibilities we may not have previously explored. Author Christina Baldwin describes working in circles with others:

> A circle is not just a meeting with the chairs rearranged. A circle is a way of doing things differently than we have become accustomed to. The circle is a return to our original form of community as well as a leap forward to create a new form of community. By calling the

circle, we rediscover an ancient process of consultation and communion that, for tens of thousands of years, held the human community together and shaped its course.[20]

Call a circle to explore and reflect, and to tap into the collective wisdom of community.

As you begin your circle conversation, suggest guidelines such as the following (these guidelines are based on my work with circles over the past twenty years, as well as recommendations from the following publications listed in the Resources section under **Collective Inquiry:** *The World Café; Wisdom Circles; Calling the Circle;* and *Dialogue and the Art of Thinking Together*):

- Listen deeply to each other—listen and speak from the heart;
- Listen with the intention of understanding;
- Allow for silence;
- Contribute your thinking and your questions;
- Suspend assumptions and allow for new possibilities;
- Honor the circle, its members, and the sacred time you create together.

This is a time of remembering, creating, and learning new ways of communicating—of living and breathing together in community. In this present time we are both experts and novices at tapping the collective wisdom of groups. We are experts because we know a great deal about how to communicate and live in community—this is encoded in our life blueprint. We are novices because society, in general, has stepped away from this deep expertise and knowing. Now it is time to remember that we have always met in circles to take counsel with others.

• Collectively Reflect and Explore
Your circle might start with these questions:

- In what ways are we currently embodying our gifts?
- What do we notice that we are learning about our gifts? What do we notice about each other regarding our gifts? What else do we need to know and learn?
- What are our assumptions (the *shoulds and shouldn'ts*) about our spiritual gifts? What did we learn from suspending our assumptions? What questions do we have about our assumptions and their effects?

- What is forming, emerging, and taking shape within us as we evolve our spiritual gifts?
- In what ways might we collectively evolve our gifts?
- What actions might we take to allow ourselves to further offer our spiritual gifts to others and all of creation? How might we amplify and support each other's actions?
- What other questions are emerging at this time?
- What are our next steps?

Preparing for Portal Two

The radiations from the fields of higher consciousness that you have showered upon yourself will begin to prepare you for the work of the second portal of the Rainbow Wheel map for conscious soul evolution. Stepping through this next portal you will bring yourself back into greater alignment with the Genesis Pattern within, as you liberate the gatekeepers of your core distortion.

6

Portal Two: Liberating the Gatekeepers

*Look inside yourself;
everything that you want,
you are already that.*
—Rumi

The invocational processes of Chapter 5 provide a way for remembering that you are already *"everything that you want"*—you *are* all of the divine gifts of creation. Invocation makes the invisible, visible—it brings this knowing to the surface, where you can embrace it. The energies of the spiritual gifts arise in your awareness. And in this process, the energies of the core distortion can be seen as well.

As you continue your practice of invocation, you will hopefully soon begin to feel the energies of the gifts building in your consciousness, and you will start to notice how your attention is more easily drawn to thinking, feeling, and acting in ways that are in alignment with this energy. You might also begin to more readily notice energies that are not in alignment with these gifts—the previously hidden energies of the core distortion. This noticing occurs as your invocation renders the invisible, visible, opening new possibilities for evolution.

The image of the dragonfly is associated with the Rainbow Wheel map's second portal of Liberating the Gatekeepers, because the dragonfly is a symbol of the power of transforming illusions. With this portal, illusions become visible because of your invocation. The illusions created by the core distortion deter you from knowing your true divine self. This portal supports you in liberating yourself from these illusions. For example, when I invoke my gift of *Peace*, its energy field helps dispel the illusion of my core distortion that "*I don't get it right.*" The truth of my gift of *Peace* helps lift the illusion of my core distortion, creating an opportunity for me to discern its effects, comprehend its origins, claim my role in its formation and continuation, and transform it into a vibrant, evolutionary energy. In choosing to invoke and liberate, you are choosing self-responsibility and evolving your soul.

The Rainbow Wheel offers a way of surfacing the energies of these illusions—invocation can have this effect. The pathway of the core distortion becomes visible and although it is in many ways simple to choose the path of the Genesis Pattern instead, it can also be quite challenging. While you may not actually *enjoy* taking the jagged-edged path created by the core distortion, it can be appealing and easy because you've done it many times before—you've become accustomed to taking this path.

Now you are at a new choice point, a choice about which path you will attend to. You know and have used both of these paths—the path of the Genesis Pattern (the interconnected circles of life), and the path of the core distortion (the jagged-edged path). In each present moment you have a choice to make. *Consciously choosing to create* for the sake of creation, and to unfold your divine presence in full form, will lift veils and reveal the universe within.

Moving Along Our Energy Pathways

There is an instructive story that author and creative process consultant Robert Fritz tells in his book *The Path of Least Resistance* that provides a useful metaphor for thinking about pathways:

> People who come to my native Boston often ask me, "How did they ever design the layout of the roads?" There appears to be no recognizable city planning in Boston. The Boston roads were actually formed by utilizing existing cow paths. But how did these cow paths come to be? The cow moving through the topography tended to move where it was immediately easiest to move … she put one foot in front of another, taking whichever step was easiest at that moment, perhaps avoiding a rock or taking the smallest incline …

Each time cows passed through the same area, it became easier for them to take the same path they had taken the last time, because the path became more and more clearly defined. Thus, the structure of the land gave rise to the cows' consistent pattern of behavior in moving from place to place. As a result, city planning in Boston gravitates around the mentality of the seventeenth-century cow.[1]

We each have our own version of the seventeenth-century cow dictating how our life-force energy moves through our internal roadways. The energy of the core distortion is the cow slowly moving, step after step after step, year after year, lifetime after lifetime, wearing in the grooves of a pathway along which your life-force energy then flows. And just as the seemingly haphazard roads of Boston can generate stress for their users, your jagged-edged pathways—the energy pathways formed by your core distortion—can constantly stress the overall system of you.

The energetic pathway of the Genesis Pattern, as discussed in Chapter 3, and seen again here in Figure 9, is a naturally manifesting pathway for you as a form of creation—it is an energetic pathway of your divine self.

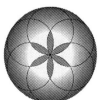

Figure 9.
The Genesis Pattern

The jagged edges of the core distortion form other pathways that become embedded in the primary pathway of the Genesis Pattern. These alternate routes take your energy off course, and interfere with the clear flow of the Genesis Pattern, as illustrated again in Figure 10. With repeated use they become what Fritz refers to as *the path of least resistance.* So every time I take the jagged-edged path of reacting to my core distortion that *"I don't get it right,"* the grooves become deeper. Every time I try to "get ahead of the curve" or "outthink" a situation or "keep things calm until I can figure out how to get it right," I'm taking the path of my own seventeenth-century cow.

Figure 10.
The Jagged Edges of the Core Distortion

Over time, I've discerned some signals that tell me when I'm on this cow path instead of the path of my gift—a path that is in alignment with the energies of the Genesis Pattern. When I feel a sense of panic or desperation, and a quivering pit in the bottom of my stomach, I now know which path I'm on. These feelings arise when I've stepped away from my center, from my deep knowing that I already *am* everything that I am seeking.

When this happens, I've learned to pause, breathe deeply, and invoke *Peace*. I shift from *reacting* to *choosing* to create, and thus I move from fragmentation and illusion to the wholeness, ease, and flow of the path of *Peace*. I can then see and experience whatever situation I'm in from the view of higher consciousness, listening for the wisdom of my true divine voice, so that I can create. I also commit to examining more about what, in that particular situation, jolted me onto one of the old cow paths so that I can continue my learning.

With invocation you are *choosing* to focus your energies on the pathway of the Genesis Pattern and the deepening of its grooves so that *it*, once again, becomes the path of least resistance. Through conscious choice and intention you change the structure of your energetic landscape: your invocation brings to you, and enlivens within you, an energetic field of higher consciousness that *is* the structure and form of the Genesis Pattern. With conscious, repeated use, this can then become the pathway that your energy follows. And just like unused cow paths, the jagged-edged trails fade away.

Invoke, Invoke, Invoke!
Liberate the Gatekeepers of Your Core Distortion

Taking the jagged-edged paths of the core distortion throughout your lifetime can be referred to as a "habit." There are many reasons why you develop habits, and this is also true for the energy habit of taking the jagged-edged path of the core distortion. In addition, primary habits often have related or supporting structures or other habits that keep them in place. I refer to these secondary habits as *gatekeepers*.

Before exploring these gatekeeper habits, let's look more closely at why the jagged-edged energy paths form at all. The energy of the core distortion and its resulting paths can form in reaction to many different types of life situations. They might start in response to life events that are fragmenting, confusing, or threatening at some level (physical, emotional, or mental). It's like receiving a jolt, either large or small, that leaves enough of an energetic imprint to form a jagged-edged pathway either overlaid on, or embedded in, your original Genesis Pattern formation.

Because the jolt was sufficient to make an indelible energy imprint, a new pathway is now available—a jagged-edged pathway, much like the impression lightning leaves in the sky. And until you dissipate the energies of these jagged-edged pathways that become embedded in the layers of your soul, they journey with your soul across lifetimes, becoming visible pathways for your energies to travel as you encounter the experiences and circumstances of the new lifetime.

As soul, you are an accumulation of all of the experiences and energies of all of the lifetimes you have lived. You are, in this present moment, made of the threads of light and the energy pathways of the creation pattern that creates you and all of the cosmos, *and* the energy pathways formed throughout *all* of your lives—you are a fabric woven of light. As your soul came into your physical body of this lifetime, the jagged-edged energy pathways of the core distortion came along as well, and when you encounter what seems to you like a fragmenting, disorienting, or threatening situation in this lifetime, you can easily begin to take those old, well-known cow paths. And new pathways might also form from new jolts.

The energies of my own core distortion ("*I don't get it right*") emerged in this lifetime in reaction to an emotionally volatile situation that was a part of my childhood. My father, who was a kind, loving, generous, and gentle person, also had a biochemical brain imbalance that created emotional turmoil for him and others: he was "bipolar." His emotional ups and downs—his cycles of sudden anger, high energy, and deep depressions—left my family "walking on eggshells." The emotional jolts formed jagged-edged pathways and exposed others that were already present in my energy field. My seventeenth-century cow paths became visible once again. And I started taking those paths of least resistance—I fell into the habit of following those grooves.

Taking these energetic pathways as you live your daily life can manifest in many different ways. Understandably, you may develop a wide range of emotional, mental, and behavioral routines and strategies for coping with life's challenges. These routines and strategies become *gatekeepers* and help to hold the energies of the jagged-edged pathways in place, creating a status quo of "you" from lifetime to lifetime. You might think of these gatekeepers as forming a tall, sturdy, borderlike fence around the jagged-edged path of the core distortion.

Some people I have worked with have reported that they've seen the gatekeepers as cartoonlike characters forming a blockade along the pathway. These gatekeeper routines and strategies may even have been perceived as being helpful to you—they may have truly supported you in dealing with life's stresses. They also have kept you on this jagged-edged pathway, acting almost like blinders as you take step after step after step. The pathway of the Genesis Pattern offers you a different type of energy—a coming home to the cosmic energy of creating, of evolving soul.

My own gatekeeper routines and strategies often have had to do with keeping conflict at bay. In my childhood I became very dedicated to methods, often subtle and refined, that would allow for bypassing conflict, like conjuring up happy distractions or anticipating an imagined potential conflict and then alleviating it before it arrived. I saw this as part of my "duty" both to myself and to the rest of my family. And a related habit that developed while I was constantly monitoring my "duty," involved "worry." I have discovered that "worry" demands continuous attention and consumes a great deal of energy.

The internal logic of my gatekeepers, which was unconscious, was that if I didn't successfully bypass or avoid conflict, then it would be because I wasn't getting it right—I wasn't doing what was "needed," so all I really had to do was figure it out! This "duty" created an unending loop of trying new ways of bypassing conflict. When the methods didn't work, the voice of the distortion said, *"I don't get it right."*

These types of gatekeepers become embedded in the energy of the Genesis Pattern formation, right along with the jagged-edged pathways, to the extent that you don't even know that these distortions and their gatekeepers exist. They simply have become a part of who you are in the world—how you think, feel, and act. They become hidden forces directing your energy and shaping the way in which you live.

The distortions become encapsulated within you, surrounded by the energies of the gatekeepers. Although you learn to work around these energy disruptions, they *do* exist and they continue to distract your attention from your spiritual gift and your evolutionary work. You are taking the path of least resistance—the core distortion's path—but it is not usually visible to you because you become shrouded in a type of fog of illusion formed by the distorted energies. The illusion is that you are not already all that you are seeking, when in fact *you are*!

So, what happens when you invoke your spiritual gift or any field of higher consciousness?

*You are lifted out of the deep grooves of the jagged-edged pathway of the core distortion and its surrounding gatekeepers, and you are **en**folded back into the pathways of higher consciousness of the void of creation. You are **en**folded back into the energy of the Genesis Pattern, the creation pattern.*

Then from the energy path of the Genesis Pattern—from your higher vision—you can claim your responsibility for the core distortion and all of its forms and arising energies. Although I am not responsible for creating my father's condition, and while behaviors and patterns I adopted may be understandable and even reasonable, I still do have responsibility for creating them and continuing to enact them throughout much of my life. In this lifetime, and previously, I created certain patterns in specific ways. Someone else in the same situation may have created entirely different patterns. The act of consciously choosing to take ownership and claim my own particular patterns and habits, allows me to bring the energies of the core distortion into my inner circle where I can mindfully learn, free myself from these energies, and transform.

When you repeatedly lift yourself into this *en*folding, learning, and creating process—when you break through and fly above the fog of illusion on the wings of the dragonfly (the symbol for transforming illusion) to your true self—you begin, once again, to naturally and joyfully take the pathway of the Genesis Pattern as you live life. It, once again, becomes the path of least resistance. Ralph Metzner reminds us in *The Unfolding Self* that "it is an ancient notion that the world perceived in our everyday consciousness is a shadow play of appearances, illusory and evanescent, and that the transformation of consciousness involves transcending or dissolving this web of images."[2] As invocation dissolves the web, your soul unfolds.

So, if you choose, **Invoke! Invoke! Invoke!** The cow paths will begin to fade away from disuse as you invoke, begin to pay conscious attention to the core distortion, and step back onto the pathway of the Genesis Pattern. As you invoke your gift and learn about the effects of the energies of the core distortion, the gatekeepers of the jagged-edged pathways—the routines and strategies—can begin to be liberated, their energies returning to the void of creation for recycling into the dance of life. And *you* will then be at a new point in your spiraling soul evolution.

What's Next?

There are two different ways in which you might continue your process at this point. Just as you earlier identified your spiritual gift, or a field of higher consciousness to which you feel drawn at this time, you can also identify your core distortion—or a primary aspect of it. Your core distortion may have a specific name or identifier, such as, *"I don't get it right."* Or it could be broader: *"Unworthiness."* However, if you decide not to work with a specific identifier for your core distortion and its gatekeepers at this time, you can continue doing your invocational practices, until a later time when you feel ready to more closely examine the energies of your core distortion.

When you enter into a practice of invocation you are intentionally choosing to transcend and transform. As was stated earlier, there are many practices suggested throughout this book that you might decide to incorporate into your practice for conscious soul evolution. If you were to choose just one, invoking your spiritual gift—or one of the other fields of higher consciousness—offers a powerful entryway for your evolution.

That said, identifying an aspect of your core distortion can bring new insights to your consciousness, supporting you on this spiraling journey. I have found it very helpful, both for myself and in my work with others. The process of identifying a primary aspect of your core distortion can make the energies less hidden, thereby providing greater opportunity for rising above the grooves.

As you continue to invoke, liberate, and leave the grooves of the jagged-edged pathways, it might feel odd, strange, or sometimes even disconcerting. For some, a new pathway can create a feeling of being lost and unsure of where to go next. For others, taking a different pathway might create a sense of excitement, much like deciding to have an adventure by taking a new route instead of the frequently traveled and well-known highway. Perhaps you will feel both excitement *and* apprehension.

Having information about your core distortion can be a support for the evolutionary process, helping to orient you as you return with clarity to the pathway of the Genesis Pattern. You may find this a good time to seek the support and guidance of counselors and healers of many different types. Lifting illusions can be disorienting. The point here is to glide back onto the road of the Genesis Pattern with the greatest ease possible rather than to create more fragmentation, disorientation, and perhaps suffering. So do what is needed to fully support yourself. Although you may still feel quite a bit in the change process, support and guidance can lead to a more ease-filled and productive transformational ride.

The following meditation is intended to assist you in identifying your core distortion, or an aspect of it. I've discovered through my spiritual mentoring work that people have their own sense of timing about when to identify and begin working with their core distortion. You may feel it is time, or not quite yet, or you might even feel a bit of both. Sometimes invocational work itself can hasten your awareness that it is time to delve into working with your core distortion. In fact, invocational work may begin to clear the fog of illusion, revealing the energies of your core distortion even if you aren't intentionally seeking them out. Radiating your energy field with the light of higher consciousness can have this effect.

I suggest that you center yourself in your Blessing Chamber and sense whether now is the time to begin this intentional part of your work with the energies of your core distortion. If you would rather not do so at this time, I suggest that you continue to read the rest of this chapter and then move on to the next chapter, which discusses the third portal of the spiraling breath. Breathwork can profoundly enhance your invocational work. And if at some time you are drawn to identify your core distortion, then you can return to do the following meditation at that time. Trust your inner knowing of what is needed for your soul's evolution in this present moment.

Identifying Your Core Distortion

There are many guided meditations, visualizations, and other types of experiences available to assist you in reaching the deep inner knowing of the higher realms. Whichever method you choose, it's important to release yourself of any preconceived notions of what your core distortion may be. Come into a neutral stance and allow yourself to experience this inner knowing, rather than "thinking" this knowing.

The Clear Light of the Heart meditation may help you with this process. It is intended to help connect you with the guiding energy of the heart. Doing so can help you stay out of your "thinking" mode and instead invite you into your heart-knowing mode. As you step into the beam of clear light in the heart, stay open to all possibilities. The instructions for this meditation follow, just as they were provided earlier, except that the specific question you are posing concerns the core distortion rather than your gift.

Also, be aware that while your focus here is on identifying the *core* distortion (as opposed to other individual layers of distortions), it can be very valuable to work with those as well. Ask to identify the core distortion, and then let go. Whatever layer of distortion you work with will affect your evolution, and if you later find a deeper layer you'll work with it then. Just as was the case with identifying your gift, your time and effort will not be lost.

As was stated earlier about *The Clear Light of the Heart* meditation, while some people may follow these instructions precisely, others might begin the meditation and then find that their experience diverges from these instructions. Some people are more visual and "see" every step as it is presented. Others are more "auditory" and begin to have experiences that are based more in sound, while others may dance, fly, or spin their way into the wisdom of the clear light of the heart. Some have a more linear experience as written here, and others may engage in a "sense" of the experience. Let this meditation unfold for you in your own particular way.

Here are the instructions for *The Clear Light of the Heart* meditation (an audio file of this meditation is available at the author's website, www.joelise.com):

Begin by lying on your back or sitting in a comfortably supported position. Close your eyes and breathe deeply to clear yourself. Breathe in through your nose and release the breath out through your mouth, cleansing yourself of all tension being held at the moment. Breathe easily and deeply, filling yourself fully with your breath—filling your lungs and your abdominal area. As you release the breath, release any tension and stress you have been holding. Take a full breath in through your nose, and release the breath out through your mouth. And when you are ready, bring your breath to a gentle and rhythmic state, changing the breath pattern to gently inhaling through your nose, and also gently exhaling through your nose. Continue to feel your body filling with the breath, your belly and chest expanding and releasing with each cycle of the breath.

Now, put your right palm on your heart. Gently breathe into your heart. See the breath flow into all of the chambers of your heart, and as you breathe see that the breath is made of pure, clear light. Feel the light filling all of the chambers of your heart, and as it does so, see your heart opening like a beautiful flower coming into full bloom. Know that you are in the center of the clear light of creation. With each breath see the light filling every fiber of your physical body and your energetic field. Also see the light moving out beyond you, filling all of the space around you with this luminous, brilliant light of creation.

Offer your gratitude for the love of this light and then send the light above and below for the benefit of All. With the inbreath, fill all of yourself with the light. With the outbreath, see the light flowing out of you to all of creation. It is moving out the top of your head—your crown chakra—to the sky, and it is flowing out the bottoms of your feet to the earth. With each complete cycle of the breath, the light fills all of you and all of creation.

Now, focus your breath on the heart, breathing the light into your heart. As you bring your attention to this heart space, state your question: **What is my core distortion?** Now, follow the light of your breath into your heart. See yourself taking a gentle walk on a pathway in the most beautiful place in all of the cosmos. Know that the light of this place will guide you. As you follow the light of your breath on this gently flowing path, you will arrive in a magnificent valley. You may be surrounded by the energy of the ancient wise trees, or rainbow gardens of light, or sacred pools of healing water, or sandy, windswept beaches. Open to receiving the beauty that surrounds you. Notice all of the life forms and take in the sounds and the fragrances.

As you reach the end of the pathway, continue moving to whatever area resonates for you, to wherever you are drawn—go wherever the light of your breath guides you. It may be similar to the pathway that brought you here, or it may be entirely different. Go to where the light of the breath leads you. You may continue walking on a path, or you may go through another opening or gateway. You may find that you move by walking or perhaps you will fly, or you might simply appear in another location. You may be in the chamber of a cave, in a pool of water, in an ocean, on a mountaintop, in a desert, or in a forest. Just follow the clear light of your breath.

You are in the center of the wisdom of the cosmos. You have stepped into a beam of cosmic light containing all—*all* of the energy and *all* of the wisdom of the cosmos. This is an ancient sacred space—an invocational field for accessing the higher realms of universal knowledge and wisdom. What is spoken, experienced, or known here is the truth of the heart. You may find the answers to your question about your core distortion with the help of a guiding energy that has a specific form, such as an animal guide, a human guide, or a guide of some other form. Or you may connect with a guiding energy that has no specific form. You may find that you simply "know" the answer to your question. The trees, the wind, the water, the air, the earth, or the light may inform you.

You may have an experience that is similar to taking a journey and you may find yourself transported to another place. Or, you may stay where you are. You may hear sounds or vibrations that communicate to you. You may sense or know things that relate to the answers to your question. Just let this unfold. You are in the center of the inner clear light of your heart, the center of all of creation. Now, ask your question: *What is my core distortion? And then let your experience unfold.*

When your experience is complete, return to the pathway that brought you into the valley. Then, follow the light of your breath back up along the pathway, back up to where we first began our journey. When you are ready, bring yourself back to the present physical realm, the present time, the present place and open your eyes.

After completing *The Clear Light of the Heart* meditation, you might, as previously suggested, consider journaling about your experiences and the information you accessed. Journaling is a way to reveal your inner wisdom and to continue working with what you experienced in the sacred space of the heart. It may help you deepen your understanding. And as you journal you may discover new questions that you would like to bring to this heart space at another time. Remember, you can always journey back to *The Clear Light of the Heart*.

The Conscious Work of Liberation

Waves of energy move through the cosmos interacting with and creating life. The cosmic waves of the fields of higher consciousness move through you and arise within you as you live life, and as you invoke them: waves of love, waves of joy, or waves of gratitude. The energy of the core distortion also arises within you as a wave that can manifest in a variety of ways: waves of panic, waves of anger, or waves of despair.

Conscious practices can help you become more aware of the ways in which these energies have become a part of your life—the form of these waves within you. The following three-step practice of ***observing, reflecting,*** and ***acting*** may help you more consciously work with the dynamics of the energy wave of your core distortion, and its gatekeepers, as you continue your invocational process.

Step 1: *Observe the indicators that you may have stepped onto the jagged-edged pathway of the core distortion.* Notice the energy wave of the core distortion moving through you and how it's manifesting. When you are stepping onto the jagged-edge path, the energy will move through you like a wave. For example, I'm aware of a wave of energy that moves through me and creates a quivering in my torso, accompanied by a feeling of impending doom, in conjunction with a sense of my "heart sinking to my stomach."

I had been aware of the sensation of this energy wave for many years, but upon closer observation I became aware that it sometimes was very subtle and other times very strong, and my tracking of this energy wave also revealed that it was there more frequently than I had realized. I began to observe and journal about the circumstances that led to these feelings and to notice my thoughts and reactions.

This process of observing and noticing involves taking a neutral stance, stepping back and recording what you detect without judgment—of yourself or others. Beginning this process by invoking a field of compassion can help release you from self-judgment as you do the work of uncovering these types of energy disruptions, so that they can be enfolded back into the void of creation to be used once again to support life.

Step 2: *Reflect on the origins of the energy wave of the core distortion.* Coming to some understandings about the origins of these waves can help you more easefully leave the path of the core distortion and realign with the path of the

Genesis Pattern. Asking questions can help you surface new understandings. You might ask these questions using *The Clear Light of the Heart* meditation:

What in this lifetime has created this energy wave of my core distortion? What purpose did it serve?

By asking these questions I was able to see that the quivering sensation of this energy wave was what you might call an early warning system for the emotional volatility of my youth. The quiver, along with the sense of doom and my "heart sinking to my stomach," let me know there was something to pay attention to in my environment. I was literally quivering from stepping onto the path of the core distortion, with these sensations then filling my energy field.

This early warning system served a purpose: it gave me the opportunity to see if "I could get it right" and head off the "up" or the "down" that I sensed was about to occur. However, this just became an unending, self-reinforcing loop that kept me on the path of the core distortion in many, many other situations beyond this scenario of my youth.

Like the well-worn paths of Boston's seventeenth-century cows, I have walked repeatedly upon this path, in this lifetime and previously, because I know it. The landscape of my energy field has been shaped and formed to lead me onto this path of least resistance. Throughout my lifetime this wave—this quiver—has arisen each time I have stepped onto the jagged-edged pathway of the core distortion, and it has reverberated throughout me.

Step 3: *Take Action: Invoke and Act.* Invocation is a core action to take when you become aware of the energy wave of the core distortion moving through you. When your indicators tell you that you've stepped onto this path, stop and invoke the field of higher consciousness of your gift, or whichever higher field you are working with. Through repeated invocation, it can become what researcher David Hawkins refers to in *Power vs. Force* as a "field of dominance." He says these fields are "exhibited by high energy patterns in their influence over weaker ones. This may be likened to the coexistence of a small magnetic field within the much larger field of a giant electromagnet."[3] The higher fields of consciousness are strong fields existing throughout the cosmos, and like the field of a giant electromagnet, they can once again become the field of dominance over your core distortion.

Next, in addition to invocation, *act*: choose other actions that will move you from a place of *reacting* from the energy of your core distortion, to *acting* to center yourself on the pathway of the Genesis Pattern. Acting will energize a pathway. Mathematical cosmologist Brian Swimme and cultural historian Thomas Berry state in *The Universe Story* that "since energy is required to sustain anything whatsoever, a decision must be made concerning what we energize in the present moment. What we choose to energize will persist and what we choose not to energize will perish."[4]

Here is a question that you might ask using *The Clear Light of the Heart* meditation to help you discern actions that will energize the pathway of the Genesis Pattern:

> *What actions might help me onto the pathway of the Genesis Pattern and create soul evolution?*

When you go into the clear light of your heart, you are able to take a higher view, to look at yourself and your life from a perspective of higher consciousness, and to know such actions.

When I took this question into my heart space, I saw the beauty of my father, and my own beauty. I also knew that to center myself on the pathway of creation and to evolve, I would need to shift my energy and release both my father and myself through a compassionate and loving soul embrace. Compassion would elevate and take me off of the path of the core distortion. In effect, the activation of this core distortion in my childhood has provided an amazing opportunity. I have been able to see the core distortion clearly now, in the present moment of this lifetime, so that *"I"* can be liberated from it for the remainder of this life and on into the next. Liberating the energy of this core distortion is giving me new energy and momentum for soul evolution.

My father's lifelong condition gave me the chance to learn and evolve: it has been a teaching and a gift for my evolution, and I believe that by the end of his life my father was also able to receive his life challenges as a gift for his evolution. Of course, there were many cycles to this process, levels of emotions and thoughts to discern and work through until I found a deeper level of compassion—compassion arising from taking responsibility for my role in creating and sustaining the patterns of my core distortion. This level of compassion was unaccompanied by fear and resentment. The process of offering deep compassion to my father, and to myself, and to opening to receive more fully the compassion my father had been offering me all of my life, has let in more of the light of my gift of *Peace*. I have had a palpable sense of walls around my heart crumbling away as I continue to find the deep being within.

Layers to Liberate

Evolution is a spiraling process that continues on as you live your life in new ways from each new point along the spiral. As you consciously work with invocation and with your core distortion you may be aware of moving through layers of energy, going deeper and deeper as you look inside yourself. This is a process of both ecstasy *and* courage—summoning your courage to do this deep work allows the ecstasy of your true self to emerge. Rumi captures this experience with these words:

You're a gold mine.
Did you know that
hidden in the dirt of the earth?
It is your turn now, to be placed in fire.
Let us cremate your impurities.[5]

Taking Flight

Following is an imagined story intended to illustrate one of the many ways you might work with the energy of your core distortion to soar into a new phase of soul evolution. I invite you to join me in sitting in a state of deep inner listening to hear the tale of this fictional person:

> *Getting beyond my core distortion has been like jumping over a chasm. I've had to step back, really step back from the edge of the chasm, so that I could run far enough to get the needed speed and momentum to successfully lift off, fly across the chasm, and get safely to the other side.*
>
> *I have only been able to do this because of all of the allies, or guiding friends and spiritual energies, that have buoyed me up and literally formed an energetic bridge across the great divide between my true self and my distorted self. It did feel like jumping across the Grand Canyon, but because of my allies I was able to do it. Even though traversing my personal Grand Canyon was quite frightening, it also was a great relief to leap, and leave behind the hold my core distortion had on me.*
>
> *My core distortion has involved a sense of failure, regret, and self-judgment. This energy of often harsh judgment was always pulling on me and affecting the energy level of my physical, emotional, and mental bodies. It had kept me locked in deep inner conflicts with myself, hindering my soul's evolution.*
>
> *Through invoking my spiritual gift, which is Coherence, I was able to see through the fog of this illusion. What was beneath it was this Grand Canyon chasm. I knew that my work, now, was to literally take flight, since that would be the only way to make it across that distance—I had to rise above. That would be how I would begin to be released from the*

energy of my distortion. I would soar across the chasm, and on the other side would be me—my divine self—without the baggage of this voice of judgment.

I held a ceremony to prepare. Sitting in the center of a circle of stones, gazing upon the fire I had made, I connected with a sense of deep knowing that I could take flight at any time, that I already was the state of being that I sought, and that I would discard the core distortion like a garment that I had been wearing. Soaring across the chasm would be the same as unfastening the hook of a cape—a covering—and letting it drop to the ground and disintegrate. The earth would absorb the energy, move it through the fire of her core, and use the energy particles to create anew. I'd be released from this burdensome energy, free to consciously engage new ways of living.

I became aware of another circle forming around me, a circle of beings—guiding beings, friends, allies. These were all very loving presences, but also very forthright. They were here to do a job, and that job was to help me across the chasm. I stood and welcomed my allies with deep gratitude.

Using my higher vision—the seeing of my inner eye—I saw myself running swiftly toward a large opening of light to the west. It looked like an arched entryway that one might see leading into a garden. As I got closer I could see that to go through the gateway of light I would have to take flight and cross the large expanse of the canyon. I felt myself lifting off the ground and saw an intricately woven cloth surrounding me.

I knew that no matter what happened, it was as it was meant to be and that the circle of my allies was holding me. Using my higher vision, I flung myself into the air and crossed the chasm, sliding right through the open entryway of light and landing with my feet firmly planted on the ground. I turned and looked back across the chasm of the canyon. There I could see a shadow of myself with the cape of the core distortion lying on the ground and fading away.

Since having had that waking dream experience, I have come to sense that the real work has just begun! I'm learning new ways of being the light of Coherence. I'm finding that this gift is like a laser beam of light that is the glue of my life matrix, the substance that binds all together and formulates life itself. Old habits that were tied to my core distortion are visible now, and I can see that their energy resonances do not match that of the field of higher consciousness of Coherence—the path I am taking. So when I see the habits, I invoke Coherence, establishing the presence of this higher field. Then I move on with living life in new ways while the energy of the habits proceeds to dissipate and fade away.

This is a process that requires vigilance, but it is such a joyful vigilance. My soul's evolution reached a new place in its unfolding spiral when I soared across that canyon. I have glimpsed the unbounded beauty and generosity of the universe. I am grateful that it is so.

Ecstasy *and* Courage

There are many ways to work with your gift as an entryway for your soul evolution—to relish the joy of the rainbow lights while also dissipating the energies of your core distortion. This is an unfolding process throughout life, and it can include many types of experiences, some purely ecstatic, others requiring the courage spoken about earlier—the courage to help you **be** the truth. In the preceding tale, the ecstasy of "unbounded beauty" was known after summoning forth and using courage.

I'd like to share with you a dream story from my own experience of evolving my gift of *Peace* that highlights how ecstasy and courage can work together for your evolution. Although these types of dreams and visions can happen to anyone at any time, you may find that it is after intending, working, and practicing for a while that they begin to unfold.

This particular dreamtime experience came to me as I was traveling with my family and visiting some incredibly beautiful places. While on this journey I intentionally opened to the deeper levels of my gift of *Peace* and then had the following dream, which had two phases:

> *In phase one I was a consultant working with a group of women to help them learn how to develop deeper-level questions for dialogue—questions that would truly take them to the core. One of the women had asked a question that was more about confirming her assumptions regarding the topic than it was about delving deeper into new possibilities.*
>
> *I was actually delighted that she asked this question because it was often just the kind that we ask—questions that attempt to confirm what we already believe rather than ones that go deeper in exploring other possibilities. We can have a tendency to stay at a surface level, but what she posed gave the group the chance to identify the assumptions embedded in the question, and then to really dig deeper. As a consultant I saw this as a great opportunity, and I was hopeful that we would be able to develop a more fruitful question.*

Then that part of the dream ended and phase two began immediately:

> *I was standing outside a cave that was an ancient sacred site. It contained a circle of stones, and inside the circle there was a round boulder that was about three feet in height and four feet in diameter. Inserted into the top of the boulder was a flat, round piece of black obsidian stone. Seekers could enter the cave, stand in the inner circle of stones, and ask their question as they peered into the obsidian stone.*
>
> *The answer to your question would come to you on the "winds of God" and the "risk" was that these winds might literally blow you away so that "you" would be "annihilated." There was only one requirement that you had to fulfill before you could ask your question: you had to say, aloud, that you were willing to take this risk. If you were, then you could ask your question and the winds would respond. My sense was that this "annihilation" was the death that one would take in order to transcend one's present evolutionary stage as part of the process of conscious evolution. However, I also knew that I must be prepared to die at every level, including the physical. Unless I accepted all of the risks, I would not be meeting the requirement. I had to be prepared to die.*
>
> *I entered the cave and stood inside the circle of stones, having decided that I was willing to take the risk on all levels. I began by stating aloud that I accepted the risk of annihilation. I felt this deep in my heart and knew that whatever happened it was as it was meant to be. I had total trust and my acceptance was genuine.*

Then just as I was about to speak my question, the dream abruptly ended as I awoke to the sound of the phone in my hotel room ringing with my wake-up call! I sat straight up in bed, knowing that I did, indeed, need to wake up to a deeper level of my question, just as I had coached the circle of women to do. As it turns out, I was really coaching myself. Although I awoke with a sense that my question was about my spiritual gift, I knew that I needed to go deeper. And in the light of day I also wanted to delve deeper into whether or not I was really ready to be "annihilated" and what that might truly mean—what it might mean, in Rumi's words, to "cremate my impurities" and become "a gold mine."

After experiencing that dream space, I went through many iterations of what my "real" question might be. I noticed that my questions shifted and changed over time—this seemed to be a spiraling process of going deeper and deeper. A few of the questions that surfaced were: *What is Peace? What is my role with Peace? What work must I do in order to **be** Peace? What does Peace have to do with my mission for this lifetime? How is Peace connected to my work as soul? What is being called* *forth about Peace for me in this lifetime? How can the energy of Peace guide my soul's evolution?* After working through layers of questions and assumptions, and learning much along the way, I came to rest in the following question:

What do I need to know about Being Peace?

This question opened my heart, and I felt a deep resonance and a higher knowing. It seemed to encompass every other question, went beyond the questions I had previously formulated, and shifted me to a place of trust in creation, including my own higher knowing—a deep trust that the absolute truth of what was needed in this present moment would be revealed. I *knew* this was the question to take to the cave.

Before going back to the cave, however, I also spent time searching deeply within myself to see if I was, at every level, really ready to let myself take the "risk" of "being annihilated," at least on whatever level that was going to occur in this moment. I knew this to be part of the transformative process—working with both destruction and creation in order to ascend beyond the current evolutionary stage—and yet I needed to sit with this prospect for a time. Although I sensed that this particular experience of annihilation would not end my physical life at the moment, I felt compelled to *truly* embrace the possibility and move into an even deeper sense of trust. Rumi speaks of this work when he writes:

Very little grows on jagged rock.
Be ground. Be crumbled, so wildflowers will come up
where you are. You've been
stony for too many years. Try something different. Surrender.[6]

To bring myself into that state of surrender, I emptied myself of all of the fears, hopes, and expectations that I could, and opened to the possibilities of creation. This all happened spontaneously once I had more fully embraced a yearning to move to my next evolutionary stage. I envisioned myself gathering all of the energies that needed to be released into a ball and then, with loving force, threw that ball into a fire to be transformed. I trusted that this evolutionary work would be for the benefit of all, including me and my circle of loved ones.

Then, through a meditative state, I brought myself back to the cave. I walked into the circle of stones and with deep and genuine intention I spoke aloud that I accepted the risk of annihilation. Then, I asked my question: **What do I need to know about Being Peace?** I had an immediate sense of being whisked out into the cosmos at which point "*I*" exploded into a galaxy. I saw and felt that I *was* the galaxy and that all of my light was spread throughout this wondrous cosmic formation.

Next, my perspective shifted, taking in the most expansive view possible and I saw that my light was spread, not only throughout the galaxy, but the entire cosmos. *"I"* went beyond this one galaxy to be infused into the whole cosmos, transcending time and place. I was formless and immersed in a blissful radiance, and I had the answer to my question. This was *Peace*—this was what it meant to **Be Peace** in all of its exuberance, love, grace, beauty, and joy.

Further, I also recognized this state of consciousness because I had experienced it before, vividly, when I journeyed to the portal of light in my youth, and subsequently as I have intentionally and consciously embraced that cosmic light. I realized that I had been having journeys filled with the essence of this state of *Peace* although I hadn't described it in that way.

I had a sense that all of my questions were answered in that exploding flash—it was clear that over time, perhaps over lifetimes, I would decipher and interpret all that I needed to know in order to embody this *Peace* at all levels and live each present moment from the oneness and fullness of the field of *Peace*. More of the illusions of the core distortion were lifted, and the divine nature of my true self was clear and flowing throughout all. I felt my connection to everything in a new and yet ancient way.

This experience was amazing, and I was ecstatic. Yet, I would not have had it without courage. Both in the dream space and in my waking meditation space I had to summon all the courage I could find, and then some, in order to take the "risk" of asking my question in the cave and being annihilated. Courage was needed even though it was the annihilation that was making room for the ecstasy. Rumi tells us that this is a process of dying so that we can truly live:

Seeds break open and dissolve in ground.
Only then do new fig trees come into being. So you
must die before you die.[7]

When you die in life—*dying before you die*—you awaken to the truth of the nature of the cosmos and of yourself. Illusion dies and you become life. The seeds of your divine life dissolve into the ground and begin to grow, and new life is born.

These experiences of courage and ecstasy push your edges—on an ongoing basis my edges are definitely being pushed! I continually ask myself questions about living all of it: the bliss and the suffering, the grief and the joy, the cosmic awareness and the tasks of daily life. The rapture of the miraculous experiences that I have had continues to burst open my consciousness, bringing me to new edges of living life now, here, formless and yet in this form, merged with the knowingness of the source of life.

So, how do I live here now in this present moment with all of it? That, I believe, is a key to our evolutionary process: bringing our transcendent experiences into the form of the sacred human *being* in this present moment on earth, this moment of being fully present in local, global, and cosmic communities of life.

Your Sacred Journey

Ultimately, *you* are the invocational field itself—*you* are the Blessing Chamber. And that is what this portal of *Liberating the Gatekeepers* is really all about. This is the process of formulating yourself as a clear, vibrant chamber of life, a light-filled vessel for creation—for the art of living a soul-infused life in each present moment. Sculpting a landscape conducive to taking the path of the Genesis Pattern is a key, and invocation is a master key for this sculpting process.

Biologist Bruce Lipton, in his book *The Biology of Belief*, speaks about an important lesson on the nature of life that was passed along to him from one of his early mentors. Lipton learned that for doing his cellular research, "when the environment was less than optimal, the cells faltered." However, if he "adjusted the environment, the cells revitalized."[8] The insight passed on to him was that the direct action of the environment has a significant effect on cells.

This is true of your energy field as well. When you take the direct action of changing your environment to support the creation pattern within, *you* become revitalized. Invocation is an action that alters your energy landscape and revitalizes you by liberating the gatekeepers and energies of your core distortion, and bringing you back to an unobstructed path of creation—the path of the Genesis Pattern. This is your sacred journey of coming to be a *Blessing Chamber* for the blessing of life.

Practices for Conscious Soul Evolution: Liberating the Gatekeepers

Integrating Practices—practices to support embracing, anchoring, and integrating the effects of conscious soul evolution.

• Invoke Your Spiritual Gift

Continue to invoke your spiritual gift, or any of the fields of higher consciousness on a daily basis. This practice will fill your field with the energies of higher consciousness and coax or nudge you onto the energy pathway of the Genesis Pattern—the pathway of creation and evolution. And, the jagged-edged pathways of the core distortion will fade away from disuse.

• Observing, Reflecting, and Acting

Engage in a conscious work process, as described in this chapter, to liberate the gatekeeper energies and dissipate the core distortion:

Step 1: Observe the indicators that you may have stepped onto the jagged-edged pathway of the core distortion.

Step 2: Reflect on the origins of the energy wave of the core distortion.

Step 3: Take Action: Invoke and Act.

• Journaling

Journal as a support for the three-step process of observing, reflecting, and acting. You might also journal about some of the questions provided in the next section (*Inquiry Practices*). References for journaling practices are provided in the Resources section at the end of the book.

• The Clear Light of the Heart Meditation

Journey to the clear light of your heart to experience more of your wisdom about your core distortion. Explore questions such as those suggested earlier:

- What in this lifetime has created this energy wave of my core distortion? What purpose did it serve?

- What actions might help me onto the pathway of the Genesis Pattern and create soul evolution?

You might also ask the questions in the *Inquiry Practices* section, or simply journey to the clear light of your heart for insight into the energies of the core distortion and what is needed to dissipate these energies for the evolution of soul.

Inquiry Practices—Individual Reflection and Exploration

Create a quiet space to reflect and explore the following, or other, questions. Or you might go for a walk in a place of beauty, or journal or engage in art practices while holding your questions. You might consider doing some breathwork to relax and enter a meditative state, travel to the clear light of your heart to explore one or more of your questions, or walk a labyrinth bringing your questions into that space with you.

• Reflect and Explore
A core purpose of a practice of inquiry is to free yourself from assumptions and beliefs (the *shoulds and shouldn'ts*) so that you can explore new possibilities, and open new gateways for your unfolding evolution. Live these questions for a while and see what emerges:

- What are the *shoulds and shouldn'ts* that arise from the energies of my core distortion?
- What do I need to know and learn about my core distortion to help me dissipate its energies?
- What has been a major insight for me about my core distortion?
- What new actions might I initiate to support my soul evolution, and to offer my gifts to others and all of creation?
- What might be some of my next steps?
- If I take the path of the Genesis Pattern, what is possible?

Sacred Circles—Collectively Reflect and Explore
When we reflect and think together, we tap into the collective wisdom of a circle of beings joining us on this journey of conscious evolution. Moving from individual to group reflection encourages us to consider possibilities we may not have explored previously. Call a circle and reflect together (the end of Chapter 5 provides further information about calling a circle).

• Collectively Reflect and Explore
Your circle might start with these questions:

- What insights have we had about the habits of our core distortions?
- What do we need to know and learn about to help us dissipate the energies of our core distortions?
- What are the *shoulds and shouldn'ts* arising from our core distortions?
- What do we notice is forming, emerging, and taking shape within us as we dissipate the energies of our core distortions?

- What actions might we take to allow ourselves to further offer our spiritual gifts to others and all of creation? How might we amplify and support each other's actions?
- What might be some of our next steps for evolution?

Preparing for Portal Three

Liberating the gatekeepers of your core distortion opens new possibilities for unfolding your soul's evolution and the creation of your life. Now as you step through the third portal of the Rainbow Wheel map for conscious soul evolution, the sacred breath of the cosmos will reinforce your work by creating a clear pathway for your continued unfolding. It will spiral throughout your physical and energetic bodies, taking you in new directions.

7

Portal Three: Spiraling Breath

*The painter of eternity
is painting images in every direction.*
—Rumi

Several years ago I was visiting a meditation center and chanting an ancient chant. It had the effect of focusing my attention on my breath, and I noticed that with each simple syllable, the rhythm of my breath was altered. Following the chant there was a meditation in which I continued to breathe consciously. While focusing on my breath it was if I could not only feel the breath moving throughout my body but could also "see" it moving in a spiral pattern, moving in every direction. It was an expansive sensation, and I felt as though the perimeter of my physical body almost did not exist—I was unified with all of the air around me in a new way.

Then surprisingly, through the vision of my "inner eye," I could see a small (about eight inches wide and eight inches high) whirling, blue-white tornado in front of me. This vortex of energy—this sacred wind—hovered there just spinning for a few moments, and then moved forward into me and swirled throughout my physical and energetic bodies. I could feel a clear pathway forming as I breathed in the wind of this swirling vortex of energy, this *Spiraling Breath*.

This breath helped clear debris left in my energy field from the jagged-edged pathways of my core distortion and its gatekeepers. As I worked with spiraling my breath, my energy field became increasingly clear and unencumbered, and the vibration of the frequency of the Genesis Pattern within me more clearly resonated once again—I could almost hear, like a chant, the hum of that pattern of creation within me. It also provided a clearer pathway for the energies of higher consciousness that I had been invoking, and as I continued to breathe with the spiraling vortex I felt infused with the rainbow lights of creation.

The third portal of the Rainbow Wheel map uses this movement of breath in a spiraling formation to support your evolutionary work. The spiral is a pattern that moves, ultimately, in every direction. And like Rumi's "painter of eternity," as you spiral your breath you too are a painter—an artist, creating your life and your eternity, filling the canvas of your life with each of your spiraling breaths. As with the spiral image of the Rainbow Wheel map, the breath moves along pathways that unfold in every direction, filling all of you, endlessly. By spiraling your breath throughout your physical and energetic bodies, you are creating your life.

The intention of this *spiral breathing* is to consciously breathe yourself forth as an evolving creation—to move your energy, to clear and deepen the pathways within you for unfolding the possibilities of creation.

Many spiritual traditions, dating back thousands of years, offer different forms of sacred breath to assist you in the conscious breathing forth of creation. Ralph Metzner, in *The Unfolding Self*, discusses the role of breath in healing: "It is often said that the power of breath, as the animating wind or *spiritus* of divine presence, is the medium through which the healing actually takes place."[1] The *Spiraling Breath* process of this third portal focuses on conscious breathing as a sacred practice for evolving your soul—breathing to clear the energetic overlays of your core distortion from the pathway of the Genesis Pattern. Consciously breathing in the sacred breath of creation serves an integral role in the evolution of soul.

There are different breath forms that can assist you (a few resources for breathwork are listed in the Resources section at the end of the book). What is most important is to find a form with which you resonate, a form that helps clear and uplift your energy, a form that supports a clear pathway for your unfolding evolution. You may find the *Spiraling Breath* meditation of the Rainbow Wheel useful for this purpose.

The *Spiraling Breath* Meditation

Whichever form of sacred breathwork you choose, each time you use the breath, do so with the intention of creating a clear pathway for your evolution as you summon the breath of creation. Here are the instructions for the *Spiraling Breath* meditation (an audio file of this meditation is available at the author's website, www.joelise.com):

Begin by lying on your back or sitting in a comfortably supported position. Close your eyes and breathe deeply to clear yourself. Breathe in through your nose and release the breath out through your mouth, cleansing yourself of all tension being held at this moment. Breathe easily and deeply, filling yourself fully with your breath—filling your lungs and your abdominal area. As you release the breath, release any tension and stress you have been holding. Take a full breath in through your nose and release the breath out through your mouth. And when you are ready, bring your breath to a gentle and rhythmic state, changing the breath pattern to gently inhaling through your nose, and also gently exhaling through your nose. Continue to feel your body filling with the breath, your belly and chest expanding and releasing with each cycle of the breath.

Now, put your right palm on your heart. Gently breathe into your heart. See the breath flow into all of the chambers of your heart, and as you breathe, see that the breath is made of pure, clear light. Feel the light filling all of the chambers of your heart, and as it does so, see your heart opening like a beautiful flower coming into full bloom. Know that you are in the center of the clear light of creation. With each breath, see the light filling every fiber of your physical body and your energetic field. Also see the light moving out beyond you, filling all of the space around you with this luminous, brilliant light of creation.

Offer your gratitude for the love of this light and then send the light above and below for the benefit of All. With the inbreath, fill all of yourself with the light. With the outbreath, see the light flowing out of you to all of creation. It is moving out the top of your head—your crown chakra—to the sky, and it is flowing out the bottoms of your feet to the earth. With each complete cycle of the breath, the light fills all of you and all of creation.

Now, focus your breath on the heart, breathing the light into your heart. As you bring your attention to this heart space, invoke the field of higher consciousness with which you have been working. Invoke this field—this gift—infusing its energy within and around you. Know that the energy of this field is everywhere: a field of light and consciousness that is a glowing, loving, nourishing, and protective cocoon for your work with the *Spiraling Breath*—breath that creates a clear pathway for your evolution.

Now as you breathe rhythmically and gently, visualize a small electric blue and luminous white tornado, or vortex of energy, spinning directly above you. You may see this as being above the crown of your head, or in front of the center of your forehead in the region of what is sometimes referred to as "the third eye." If you are lying down you might see this vortex above your heart or your midsection or solar plexus. Wherever it is, focus on the vortex and its spinning motion. Notice the swirling energy lines and feel the pulse and rhythm of its energy. This whirling spiral is formed by the sacred winds—*the breath*—of creation.

Invite this whirling being into your core. Welcome it with *Gratitude* and *Love*. If you feel any fear, trepidation, or anxiety, take a deep breath and acknowledge what you feel. Then, let yourself know that all is well and that this whirling being of light is a healing gift from the source light of the cosmos. Release your deep breath and release any fears or anxieties. Move to a higher state of *Gratitude* and *Love* and allow the presence of the source light of creation to fill you.

As the whirling sacred wind moves throughout your field, continue to offer your *Gratitude* and *Love* as it spirals through all of your physical and energetic bodies. As it spirals it will have a rhythm and a pulse. Align your breathing with this pulse. As the whirling, spiraling sacred wind pulses through you, allow your breath to follow the rhythm that you feel. This will be different for each person—you will know the breath rhythm that is just right for you. It is your *Spiraling Breath*, unique to you, your consciousness, and your evolutionary path. It is the breath of your soul in this present moment.

As the electric blue and luminous white tornado moves through you with your *Spiraling Breath*, a pathway for your evolution is being cleared. Follow the breath and follow the spinning vortex of energy. When it is time, the whirling vortex will rise and move back into the cosmic ethers. Your breath will change into whatever rhythmic form is needed now. Offer your *Gratitude* and *Love* to the sacred *Spiraling Breath* and to the source light of the cosmos. And when you are ready, open your eyes and bring yourself back to this present time and place.

Your breathwork will be exponential. Each practice session will build on all of your previous work. You can return to this workspace of the *Spiraling Breath* at any time, summoning this whirling vortex of energy to clear your energy pathways. You may also find it helpful to have a way of processing and reflecting on what you have experienced with the breath, patterns of which you have become aware, and anything else that you notice. The processing form you choose might be journaling, visual art, creating music, gardening, or walking. There are a variety of ways to enter into a reflective process. Be aware of new arisings from the depths of your consciousness, and be awake to the ways in which the conscious sacred breath is affecting you. Notice how the breath and your energy are moving as you more fully come into your true center—*your divine self.*

Breathing Away the Ice

I invite you once again to join me at the hearth, around the fire, to hear an imagined tale about the powers of sacred breath for this fictional person:

> *My story is about ice, and here's what happened. Several years ago while on a journey, I had the great fortune of meeting a very wise, elder man. He was kind and gentle, and seemed to have great inner balance and peace. I envied this man who moved with such grace. While I realized that having envy was not a good state to be in, the truth of it was that the envy was there. This man, this teacher, could sense my internal struggle with envy, so he took it upon himself to offer a productive way for me to wrestle with this condition. He invited me to stay with him for a time, which was not defined, and to work for him in exchange for room and board. The land around this man's home was beautiful, the work would involve physical labor, which I enjoy, and I had time. I welcomed this opportunity to learn, so I stayed.*
>
> *The first few weeks were very peaceful and relaxing. We started each day with a silent walk in the nearby woods or in the meadow behind the house. In silence he led and I followed. At times, following his lead, we stepped very gently and quietly while other times we took quick, brisk steps. I started to notice my breathing during these walks, and I also observed his breathing. What I discovered was that his breathing was always the same, no matter how slow or fast we were moving. He seemed to have an internal rhythm dictated by something other than the happenings of his physical body. I asked him how he had come to be able to breathe in this way, but he said that answering that question directly wouldn't help me. He said that I had to find my own answer as to how to breathe with the rhythm of the universe.*
>
> *I suddenly knew why I was there, why I had taken this journey and stayed with this man. It was time for me to learn how to breathe fully, to connect with the fullness of the life-force energy—the chi of the universe—and the breath within me that carries that energy. Learning to breathe, really breathe, would expand all of the possibilities of life, and my evolution would soar.*
>
> *The next few weeks were more rigorous and intense. We worked on building a round, partially earth-sheltered room that was to be used as a*

meditation space. My host and mentor had begun this project but hadn't gotten very far yet. Winter was quickly approaching and he hoped to have it completed by then, so we worked daily from sunup until late into the evening. This man's endurance was astonishing. Here I was at least fifty years younger, and I needed to stop before he did! When I asked how he did it, he said, "Clear breath." As we worked each day I contemplated that phrase, "Clear breath." However, while I contemplated and worked it seemed that I only became more and more envious, and I noticed that my breath wasn't aligning with the rhythm of the universe. If anything, it was becoming more labored.

One day I was so frustrated that I put down my tools and went for a walk by myself. I went to the meadow and just started walking in ever widening circles. After a while I heard crows cawing. I stopped, and looking up I saw several crows circling above me. It seemed that they were tracing the lines of my circles, and their calls felt as though they were mocking me. Then, much to my surprise, I sat down and began to weep. I wept until I was exhausted, and I lay down, absorbing the warmth of the sun and being refreshed by the cool breeze blowing over me. I fell asleep and began to dream.

In my dream, one of the crows landed and walked over to me. In its mouth it had an ice pick. I couldn't imagine why a crow would have such a thing, but that was very clearly the case. It laid the ice pick in my hand and communicated words to me. I didn't hear words, but I knew what the crow was communicating—I knew its message. It told me that I needed to take a higher view, but that I was weighed down by all of the cold blocks of ice in my veins. The crow said that because of the ice, neither my blood nor my breath could flow on its natural course.

The cold blocks of ice were energy blockages from old hurts, old wounds, and old limiting thoughts and beliefs. Envy was one of the blocks of ice. The crow said that I could dissolve those blocks with the ice pick of breath. All I needed to do was see the edges of the breath moving through all of the energy lines of my body and that those edges would break through the ice, clearing the way for the light and life-force energy of the universe to flow through me as intended. Then the dream ended and I awoke with a start and also with a sense of peace.

I spent the next months of winter working with the edges of my breath, clearing the blocks of ice. During that time I designed a garden to sculpt and create in the spring. It would go right outside the meditation room my host and I had finished. That design process also helped *with clearing the ice. It was a process of creating a physical environment that was in flow, and so I was working with flow both internally and externally. By the time the garden was planted I knew that the breath of life was creating my life in each and every present moment. I worked through many layers of ice, and while I know there is still more work to be done, I also know that the breath of life will guide me in my evolution and my soul will soar.*

Your Sacred Journey

Through the Rainbow Wheel map for conscious soul evolution you have been engaging in a process of coming to know your gift (or another field of higher consciousness), and also to know your core distortion. These energies have been a part of the story of you. This is the story of your gift that is woven into the light fabric of your soul, and the story of your core distortion as an overlay of disruptive energy onto that fabric of light. Now with your sacred breathwork you are clearing away remaining debris and energy imprints of the core distortion so that you can once again know, with clarity, the truth of the story of your divine self—the story of you as creation.

Professor and management theorist Peter Senge, in *Presence: Human Purpose and the Field of the Future*, shares an experience he had in Egypt about creation stories: "I was in Egypt recently, visiting the new library of Alexandria. The old library was a powerful symbol for the gathering and sharing of human wisdom, and the Egyptian government hopes the new library will re-create that purpose … All along the concrete facade, the creation stories from ancient traditions around the world are engraved in their own script." Senge goes on to say that he believes "our willingness to hold and consider different stories can free us from being isolated in our own."[2]

Like the new library of Alexandria, you are a depository of stories. This work of the sacred conscious breath offers a way of helping to free yourself from the isolation of the story of your core distortion. Instead, you can reunite with your own original creation story, in your own script—the story of *you* as a part of the gift of the whole of creation.

Practices for Conscious Soul Evolution: Spiraling Breath

Integrating Practices—practices to support embracing, anchoring, and integrating the effects of conscious soul evolution.

• Invoke Your Spiritual Gift
Continue to invoke your spiritual gift, or any of the fields of higher consciousness. Make this a daily practice.

• The *Spiraling Breath* Meditation or Other Breathwork
Use the meditation provided earlier in this chapter to spiral your breath, or other forms of breathwork to clear the way for the energy and light of the field of higher consciousness of your spiritual gift to flow throughout all of you. References for breathwork are provided in the Resources section at the end of the book.

• Journaling
Reflect and write about your experiences with the sacred conscious breath. You might journal about some of the questions suggested in the following *Inquiry Practices* section. References for journaling practices are listed in the Resources section.

• Art
Engage in art practices that help you explore your experience with breath and with the flow of the field of your gift throughout all of your form and being: drawing, painting, creating a collage, beading, making or coloring a mandala, composing a song, sculpting, dancing, etc. References for creating art are listed in the Resources section.

Inquiry Practices—Individual Reflection and Exploration
Create a quiet space to reflect and explore the following, or other, questions. Or you might go for a walk in a place of beauty, or journal or engage in art practices while holding your questions. You might consider doing some breathwork to relax and enter a meditative state, travel to the clear light of your heart to explore one or more of your questions, or walk a labyrinth bringing your questions into that space with you.

• Reflect and Explore
A core purpose of a practice of inquiry is to free yourself from assumptions and beliefs (the *shoulds and shouldn'ts*) so that you can explore new possibilities and

open new gateways for your unfolding evolution. Live these questions for a while and see what emerges:

- As I spiral breath through my form and being, what do I notice? What arises? What images do I see? What do I feel? What do I know?
- What within me is changing? What is being healed and cleared?
- Are there new insights emerging from my breath practice? What is forming, emerging, and taking shape within my center?
- What assumptions have surfaced (the *shoulds and shouldn'ts*) while working with the breath?
- What might be some next steps for my evolution?

Sacred Circles—Collective Reflection

When we reflect and think together, we tap into the collective wisdom of a circle of beings joining us on this journey of conscious evolution. Moving from individual to group reflection encourages us to consider possibilities we may not have explored previously. Call a circle and reflect together (the end of Chapter 5 has further information about calling a circle).

• Collectively Reflect and Explore
Your circle might start with these questions:

- What have we noticed about our breathwork?
- What within us is changing?
- Is there a new awareness emerging from our breath practice? What is forming, emerging, and taking shape?
- As we've done our breath practices, have we noticed any assumptions (the *shoulds and shouldn'ts*)? What questions do we have about our assumptions and their effects?
- What might be some of our next steps for evolution?

Preparing for Portal Four

The first three portals of the Rainbow Wheel map for conscious evolution support you in gliding back onto the path of the Genesis Pattern—life's energy pattern. Now as you move on to stepping through the fourth portal you will more fully renew and revitalize this pathway within. This renewal can change the way in which you go about creating and living your life, indeed transforming the ground field—the basis—on which you connect with all of the cosmos. Rumi captures the essence of this in the following poem:

At night, I open the window and ask
The moon to come and press its
face against mine. Breathe into
me. *Close the language-door and*
open the love-window. The moon
won't use the door, only the window.[3]

8

Portal Four: Renewing the Genesis Pattern

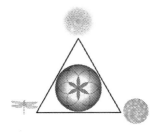

*Like a lily, we open up
and unravel from ourselves.
Like a flowing stream,
we go from one garden to the next.*
—Rumi

My daily practices helped dissipate the energies of my core distortion. As I did this soulwork and the fog lifted, another related energy distortion became visible. I came to realize that it had occurred as a consequence of having lived with my core distortion ("*I don't get it right*") for a long time—many lifetimes. The newly identified pattern involved an awareness of feeling pulled in many different directions. I had a deep sense of fragmentation that had developed from continuously seeking another way, as I attempted to "get it right."

As a result of invoking my gift, liberating the gatekeepers, and spiraling breath, I was ready for a new level of embracing the oneness of creation. I had previously experienced this state when connecting with the whirling rainbow lights and when I had exploded into the entire cosmos upon asking what I needed to know about being *Peace*. Now I felt called to invoke the field of *Unity* and to move beyond the illusion of fragmentation. My sense was that through invoking *Unity* I would amplify what I had learned through my previous encounters with cosmic light, and would have greater ease in bringing that knowing into an enduring state of consciousness.

One night, after having spent several weeks focusing on the invocation of *Unity*, I was suddenly awakened, and although completely awake I was also aware of being in a deep meditative state. In this state I was able to use my higher vision to see myself standing on the earth under a cloudy, yet luminous sky. I was aware that I was "hearing" the thunder of the heavens and "seeing" waves of heavenly lightning—the sacred light of creation. Suddenly, the sky opened up and a thick bolt of lightning came crashing down and struck the earth next to where I was standing. It stayed there, connecting heaven and earth. *"I"* stepped onto the lightning bolt and walked up into the heavens.

Once I was above the clouds the lightning bolt receded and the clouds closed. I saw that above the clouds everything was infused with a field of electric blue light. I voiced my intention of merging into a state of oneness with this radiant light, and almost immediately I had a sense of vibrating and felt myself *become* the electric blue light. *"I"* didn't exist, and yet I was more fully present than ever before. The clouds parted again and I walked back down the bolt of lightning to stand in a magnificent garden with a flowing fountain of light in the center. I stood as the witness to this light, and saw that *"I"* was the light of the fountain—always flowing, always luminous, always one with creation. I had stepped back onto the pathway of the Genesis Pattern and had renewed my sense of oneness with creation.

Renewing the Genesis Pattern is a process of coming home to the wondrous beauty in the center of the garden of life, the garden of your soul. Lilies, which Rumi uses in the poem at the beginning of this chapter, often symbolize spiritual enlightenment, peace, transcendence, openheartedness, spiritual ecstasy, and rebirth. And the center of the Genesis Pattern, seen in Figure 11, is just like that open lily—calling you to unravel yourself from its center and consciously step back onto the path of the Genesis Pattern and the flow of creation.

Working with the four portals of the Rainbow Wheel map is a means for coming to this place of the center of the garden of life. This place is your heart space and the center of your soul. This center connects you to the sacred source light of all of the fields of higher consciousness. When you enter the heart space, you journey to a realm that is a connecting fiber, linking together all realms of the source light of creation. It's like stepping into a corridor that reaches all of the dimensions and realms of the cosmos, much like the oceanic bodies of water that connect all of the continents of the earth: once you enter into the stream of water you can travel anywhere.

Figure 11.
The Genesis Pattern:
Symbol for the Energy Formation of Creation

The intention of the first three portals—*Invoking Your Spiritual Gift, Liberating the Gatekeepers,* and *Spiraling Breath*—is to bring you more deeply into your heart space and the center of your soul. Now with the fourth portal you can consciously choose to begin a process of fusing yourself back onto the energy pathway of the Genesis Pattern, renewing it as your primary path for the journey of life. Through fusion you reunite with the creation pattern within.

Different types of ceremonies and meditation experiences, as well as spontaneous spiritual openings, might bring you to this place of fusing with the pathway of the Genesis Pattern. Invoking *Unity* and experiencing a cosmic bolt of lightning helped me to fuse back onto this pathway. Rumi describes such transformational, sacred light:

There is light that can shatter this earth-and-sky.
It cannot be seen with eyes.[1]

This light is shattering, transforming what has been, and yet not visible with your human eyes—it is beyond your normal sight. This is the luminous, pulsating, shimmering light of creation that can fuel the next step of your spiraling evolution, of your soul's life here in this present moment of you as a human *being.*

Perhaps you will begin your conscious fusion process while gazing at the stars or walking in a favorite place. This will most likely not be a one-time experience. Remember, this is a continuously unfolding, spiraling process. I find that as I continue to work through layers and round new turns in my evolutionary spiral, I fuse with the Genesis Pattern from my new present place.

Meditation for Renewing the Pathway of the Genesis Pattern

The following *Clear Light of the Heart* meditation offers a way to begin this process of fusing with the pathway of the Genesis Pattern. You may find it helpful either on its own or in conjunction with other methods. The purpose of this work, whichever method you choose to aid you, is to journey to the center of your heart and renew the Genesis Pattern within you as the primary path for your journey in this lifetime. This guided meditation involves consciously and intentionally fusing with the energy pathway of this creation pattern within, through calling the light of creation to shift you. Just like a bolt of lightning electrifies and alters the air and the earth, in this meditation the sacred light of creation offers an energy charge that can reunite you with the pathway of the Genesis Pattern.

Here are the instructions for this guided meditation (an audio file of this meditation is available at the author's website, www.joelise.com):

Begin by lying on your back or sitting in a comfortably supported position. Close your eyes and breathe deeply to clear yourself. Breathe in through your nose and release the breath out through your mouth, cleansing yourself of all tension being held at this moment. Breathe easily and deeply, filling yourself fully with your breath—filling your lungs and your abdominal area. As you release the breath, release any tension and stress you have been holding. Take a full breath in through your nose and release the breath out through your mouth. And when you are ready, bring your breath to a gentle and rhythmic state, changing the breath pattern to gently inhaling through your nose, and also gently exhaling through your nose. Continue to feel your body filling with the breath, your belly and chest expanding and releasing with each cycle of the breath.

Now, put your right palm on your heart. Gently breathe into your heart. See the breath flow into all of the chambers of your heart, and as you breathe see that the breath is made of pure, clear light. Feel the light filling all of the chambers of your heart, and as it does so, see your heart opening like a beautiful flower coming into full bloom. Know that you are in the center of the clear light of creation. With each breath see the light filling every fiber of your physical body and your energetic field. Also see the light moving out beyond you, filling all of the space around you with this luminous, brilliant light of creation.

Offer your gratitude for the love of this light and then send the light above and below for the benefit of All. With the inbreath, fill all of yourself with the light. With the outbreath, see the light flowing out of you to all of creation. It is moving out the top of your head—your crown chakra—to the sky, and it is flowing out the bottoms of your feet to the earth. With each complete cycle of the breath, the light fills all of you and all of creation.

Now, focus your breath on the heart, breathing the light into your heart. As you bring your attention to your heart space, state your intention to journey to **the clear light of your heart, to fuse with the pathway of the Genesis Pattern.**

Then, follow the light of your breath into the center of the garden—the center of your soul. Just follow the light of your breath into the clear light of your heart.

As you follow the breath into the center of the garden of your soul, you may see either a brilliant electric-blue light or an electric-white light. Or you may see lightning around, or perhaps you will find yourself surrounded by a column of vibrating, electrified golden, white, or electric-blue light. There are many ways in which the sacred light of creation may appear to you, so just let it unfold.

This is your unique journey of fusing with the cosmic light here in physical form. You might step into the light, or onto the light, or the light might surround and infuse you. You have called forth the presence of the light of creation to fuse you into the path of the Genesis Pattern within. Now simply allow this journey to unfold.

When your experience is complete, follow your breath back up to the present physical realm, the present time, the present place, and open your eyes.

As with previous *Clear Light of the Heart* meditations, you might find journaling about this experience to be a helpful way of reflecting upon, processing, and integrating this energy. Consider journaling about words you received, visual images you saw, impressions you had, or simply what you came away *knowing*. It may also be useful to you to continue a reflective journaling process for a while. Notice and reflect upon what you feel and know, changes you may be experiencing, and the questions you have about your path, and creation. You've entered the clear light of your heart, and as Rumi says:

The clear bead at the center changes everything. [2]

Taking Action

The Clear Light of the Heart meditation guides you to speak your intention clearly and to make a conscious choice to open to this fusion process. Perhaps in doing this meditation you will have a sense of fusing, or it might be that the act of meditating opens you to this possibility, which will then occur at a different time, in your own unique way. So stay alert and look for the moment when the opportunity opens for this type of fusion. Following is an imagined story that illustrates such renewal unfolding for a fictional character:

> *My story is very simple, although it has taken me a while to get to the point of seeing and appreciating this simplicity. Sometimes pathways can seem to be strewn with a combination of deep holes and steep boulders that appear to make this evolving journey too complex. I think that*

is often just an illusion, albeit a powerful illusion that can stop one from taking the next step on that pathway.

For me, the deep holes were about an inner sense of deficit—that I had deficits I could not overcome. The steep boulders were my fears: a fear that I didn't know how to get to the state of wholeness that I was seeking, and a fear that my sense of fragmentation would impair my ability to find my way along the path.

One day, for whatever reason, I was ready to awaken to a new level. I didn't know this when I started my day, but now reflecting back, I can see how everything just fell into place. I had, for quite some time, been yearning to lift the veil of illusion. I was yearning for a greater sense of wholeness and to be freed from my imagined "deficits" and sense of fragmentation. "I" was calling forth a state of wholeness in which I might come to better know my true, divine self. And yet, I feared all of this as well. This created a never-ending push-pull effect on my spirit and my psyche. It's strange to fear the very thing one yearns for, and yet I think this is a common condition.

On this day late in summer I was presented with a window of opportunity. A client for whom I was working needed me to delay my work and reschedule. Here was this beautiful, crystal-clear day and I was open. Reflecting back, I now realize just how open I really was! I felt compelled to be outside in gardens, so I decided to go to the arboretum. It was beautiful, with every shade of blooming flower imaginable. I felt Grace present as I walked the paths and as I sat and experienced the beauty all around me. I closed my eyes, taking in the fragrances and the sounds, which included the sound of a large water fountain. I opened myself to being immersed in the Grace of this present moment. I summoned Grace and held the intention of being open.

Suddenly, I saw myself, in my mind's eye, sitting right in the center of the fountain with the water washing over me. I was being cleansed and regenerated, and I could feel every cell of my body coming alive. This sensation went beyond my physical self, and I could feel the energy waves of my whole self. As the water cascaded down around me, all of my energy was awakening, and then I knew: I was indeed whole. I could feel all of myself as being present in the moment—the water had awakened my sense of Presence. I opened my eyes and looked straight up. The blazing sun and the sparkling, radiant blue sky seemed to activate something in my heart and I felt an opening within as sun and sky seemed to descend upon me, infusing me with radiance. In that moment, I knew I was one with All. Grace had brought me to a knowing of wholeness.

As I look back upon this day, I realize that what allowed this experience and this knowing to unfold, was that I took action. I took the initiative. I responded to my yearning by going to the gardens of the arboretum. Once there, I took action again. I sat in stillness and silence, which turned out to be one of the most important actions of my life.

Your Sacred Journey

Renewing the Genesis Pattern is a process of coming into the center of the garden of creation—the garden of your soul—and fusing with higher consciousness. By consciously working with this renewal process, you will have initiated an action that will further your evolutionary path. The pacing of each soul's spiral path will be unique, leaping and changing with its own rhythm. In this spiraling process of invocation, liberation, breath, and renewal, each turn of the spiral presents a new threshold to be transcended, a new gateway for potential transformation. Each new turn of the spiral offers a new place, a new way of being, from which you can live life.

With each of these thresholds there is an intertwining and merging of all of the spiritual gifts, and all of the gifts are enlivened within you. You are a being of *The Light of Creation, Beauty, Gratitude, Breath, Ascension, Compassion, Unity, Harmony, Joy, Coherence, Peace, Love,* and *Grace*. You are an offering to *All*. May this journey to the center of your soul be blessed with the type of brilliance that Rumi describes:

In the middle of my heart,
a star appeared,
and the seven heavens were lost
in its brilliance.[3]

Practices for Conscious Soul Evolution: Renewing the Genesis Pattern

Integrating Practices—practices to support embracing, anchoring, and integrating the effects of conscious soul evolution.

- **Invoke Your Spiritual Gift**

Continue to invoke your spiritual gift, or any of the fields of higher consciousness. Make this a daily practice.

• *The Clear Light of the Heart* Meditation
Use the meditation provided earlier in this chapter to fuse with the energy of the pathway of the Genesis Pattern. You can use this meditation to journey to the Clear Light of the Heart at any time to continue to nudge yourself into the next level of this fusion process.

• Journaling
Reflect on and write about your experiences with this meditation. You might journal about some of the questions following in the *Inquiry Practices* section. References for journaling practices are provided in the Resources section at the end of the book.

• Art
Engage in art practices that help you explore your experience with this fusion and the evolution of your soul: drawing, painting, creating a collage, beading, making or coloring a mandala, composing a song, sculpting, dancing, etc. References for creating art are listed in the Resources section.

Inquiry Practices—Individual Reflection and Exploration
Create a quiet space to reflect and explore the following, or other, questions. Or you might go for a walk in a place of beauty, or journal or engage in art practices while holding your questions. You might consider doing some breathwork to relax and enter a meditative state, travel to the clear light of your heart to explore one or more of your questions, or walk a labyrinth bringing your questions into that space with you.

• Reflect and Explore
A core purpose of a practice of inquiry is to free yourself from assumptions and beliefs (the *shoulds and shouldn'ts*) so that you can explore new possibilities and open new gateways for your unfolding evolution. Live these questions for a while and see what emerges:

- What are ways in which I experience and know the ground field of the spiritual light of creation?

- Have any assumptions surfaced (the *shoulds and shouldn'ts*) while working with fusing with the energy of the spiritual light of creation—the Genesis Pattern?
- As I enter the clear bead of the center of my heart, what do I notice has changed? What thresholds have been transcended? What thresholds are calling to me to be transcended next?
- What actions might I take to allow me to further offer my spiritual gift to others and all of creation?
- What might be some next steps?

Sacred Circles—Collective Reflection

When we reflect and think together, we tap into the collective wisdom of a circle of beings joining us on this journey of conscious evolution. Moving from individual to group reflection encourages us to consider possibilities we may not have explored previously. Call a circle and reflect together (the end of Chapter 5 provides further information about calling a circle).

• Collectively Reflect and Explore

Your circle might start with these questions:

- What are ways in which we experience and know the ground field of the spiritual light of creation?
- Have we noticed any assumptions surface (the *shoulds and shouldn'ts*) while working with the higher spiritual realms?
- As we have entered our centers, what do we notice has changed? What thresholds have been transcended? What thresholds are calling to be transcended next?
- What actions might we take to allow ourselves to further offer our spiritual gifts to others and all of creation? How might we amplify and support each other's actions?
- What are our next steps?

Continuing Your Practices

Soul evolution is an ongoing process. You move through stages, continuously unfolding new possibilities for life—creating for the sake of creation. The four portals of the Rainbow Wheel map for conscious soul evolution offer you a spiraling pathway for this unfolding. Now as you continue to do the practices of these four portals, the light of your soul will become clearer and more radiant.

PART III
What's Next on the Rainbow Wheel Pathway?

○ ○

The Rainbow Wheel offers a pathway for evolving **presence**—for bringing the presence of Spirit, the deep divine within, into full form as you. Now, as you continue the conscious evolutionary practices of the four portals of the Rainbow Wheel map, you will advance your journey of eliciting and enacting the presence of Spirit in you, fully engaging yourself as the *Sacred Human Being*.

Make the most of this single breath called life.

—Rumi

9

Your Spiritual Ancestry

You arrived in this lifetime with a spiritual ancestry that provides a foundation for your life and your continued evolutionary work. It is a force impacting the unfolding of this lifetime. Through your spiritual ancestry you brought with you creation's blueprint, all of your soul's energy imprints, and your connection to the collective of all souls. Your spiritual ancestry is all that is known by "you" in this present moment of life, and it is key to the evolutionary work of this lifetime. It helps to shape this present moment of *Spirit* being human, and human being *Spirit*, in the form of *you*.

Taking a closer look at your spiritual ancestry can assist you in your ongoing work with the portals of the Rainbow Wheel map and your awakening of presence in this lifetime. Insights from your spiritual ancestry can come in many different forms. Small, seemingly insignificant observations about yourself may lead to a profound understanding about an energy pattern that has been a part of your spiritual ancestry for ages. Perhaps an experience of either anger or love will trigger cascading insights about the possibilities for your evolution. Or a powerful direct experience, whether in the waking state or the dream state, may inform your knowing of a pattern deeply embedded in your energy matrix, opening an evolutionary opportunity for this lifetime.

Sometimes these revelatory experiences come during difficult moments of life, as was the case for me. A very challenging situation opened my knowing that I had an extraordinary opportunity to shift very deep and old energy patterns that I felt as if I might have been enacting for lifetimes. Difficult moments such as these are often enormous gateways for evolution if you can allow yourself to experience the transformative possibilities of the fire of that moment. Rumi gives us this advice:

*If you stay away from fire, you'll
be sour, doughy, numb, and raw. You
may have lovely, just baked loaves
around you, but those friends cannot
help.* You *have to feel oven fire.*[1]

At age thirty-two, in a moment of receiving a challenging piece of information about my health, I spontaneously stepped into that fire.

While my husband sat in the doctor's waiting room with our three-month-old son, I was told that I had multiple sclerosis (MS). Upon hearing these words time slowed down until it seemed to stop. While I could see the doctor's lips moving and vaguely hear his voice off in the distance, my entire attention had shifted to a portal that had opened above me. "*I*" rose above my physical body, speeding through that open gateway, transported to an entirely different dimension in the heavens. I was in a crystal city in the sky filled with shimmering, whirling rainbow lights. The city was literally constructed from crystals—enormous crystal columns, crystal floors, and skylights of crystal glass. It was absolutely magnificent, and I felt both calm and ecstatic.

I had a sense of inner peace and deep understanding about my life path and knew that an old energy pattern was unfolding in this physical life. I was "remembering": I could taste familiarity, and hear its sounds as a well-known inner vibration. I could feel myself awakening, this news about my physical body nudging me toward the completion of old cycles and patterns, opening new possibilities for the evolution of my soul. It was as if I could *see* the deeply embedded patterns that I could liberate myself from in this lifetime—ancient patterns that I now know were based in grief and fear. Sensing the vibration of these patterns opened a major transformational opportunity.

I also remembered that I *am* all of the divine resonances of the shimmering, whirling rainbow lights, and I carry with me all of the possibilities of creation. I sensed this was exactly the perfect time—this lifetime and this moment—to begin to open, transform, and move to a new stage of my evolution. Then I was once again back in my body, with time regaining its normal pace.

In describing this experience, and its relationship to spiritual ancestry, I have found myself coming face to face, once again, with the challenges of putting into language what has been gathered and learned from my direct experiences of cosmic light and Spirit. In exploring this, I've found the words of scholar Joseph

Campbell to be helpful. In his renowned interview with Bill Moyers, *The Power of Myth*, Campbell explained that "the ultimate mystery of being is beyond all categories of thought. As Kant said, the thing in itself is no thing. It transcends thingness, it goes past anything that could be thought. The best things can't be told because they transcend thought. The second best are misunderstood, because those are the thoughts that are supposed to refer to that which can't be thought about. The third best are what we talk about."[2]

Given that I am engaging here in doing the third best thing, I will do *my* best to describe some glimmers of understanding—some hints—about three components of spiritual ancestry that I've gleaned from my direct experiences with the crystal city, the Rainbow Wheel, dreamwork, and other such encounters.

I've come to understand three components of spiritual ancestry:

- *Spirit's Creation Imprint*—the Genesis Pattern, carrying all of the possibilities of creation;

- *Your Soul's Energetic Matrix and Library*—the energy imprint that has been formulated through all of the generations of your soul's life, from each of the lifetimes you've had in the material, physical world and from transits through the realms of the nonmaterial, "invisible" world;

- *Your Connection to the Collective Soul Matrix*—a cosmic community of consciousness, woven from all of the threads of light of all souls.

These components can be described as follows:

Spirit's Creation Imprint—The Genesis Pattern: Your spiritual ancestry includes the energy explosion that created the cosmos and released the energies and elements necessary to create all forms of life. Cosmologist Brian Swimme and cultural historian Thomas Berry, in *The Universe Story*, eloquently describe this first explosion of the cosmos as the "primordial flaring forth" and the "originating power" that gave birth to the universe. They explain that all actions are "powered by the same numinous energy that flared forth at the dawn of time."[3]

These energies and elements of the "flaring forth" eventually formed the celestial bodies—nebulas, stars, planets, suns, asteroids, comets, solar systems, and galaxies. The same energies and elements released in the first "flaring forth" led to the formation of Earth and all of her associated life-forms. You truly are the stuff of the stars—body, mind, and soul. You are the breath and light of Spirit. *You* are a celestial body.

Spirit is the source light and source energy of all, creating and infusing all of the cosmos, providing the substance for all possibilities and all manifestations. Celestial bodies and their associated forms of life, such as you, are aggregates of energy united and blended together. Through the many forces and processes of the cosmos, the light and energy of creation—substances of Spirit—have fused together into matter, taking form in you. And having originated from the light and energy of Spirit, you contain the blueprint of Spirit—*the Genesis Pattern*—and all that arises from it. The pulsating waves of Spirit continuously inform and fuel this blueprint of life.

Your Soul's Energetic Matrix and Library: Your soul's energetic matrix is woven from the energy of light—the threads of creation. You can think of this matrix as a tightly packed web of light with many intersecting lines and points, like a grid you may have drawn in a math class. And the consciousness of Spirit is infused into this evolving matrix that is cohesively woven together into a beam of luminous, vibrating, and radiating light. Your intentional work with these threads of light of your soul matrix is generative—they are created and purified. Like a weaver spinning fine silk threads into a wave of luminous cloth, you are transforming the light of Spirit into the threads of the fabric of your soul. Three interrelated aspects comprise this matrix:

> 1. *The Material and Immaterial Realms:* The energetic soul matrix exists both in the material realm, when it manifests in a body, and in the nonmaterial realms—other dimensions that we sense and respond to, rather than "see" with our ordinary vision. Have you ever looked into someone's eyes and felt that you were seeing their soul—their spark of life? And conversely, you may have also encountered people that have seemed lifeless, as if they had "lost touch" with Spirit, with soul. Both of these are examples of ways in which we experience and know the immaterial realm. We are continuously weaving together these two realms—the material and the immaterial—to create our lives in this present moment.

> 2. *The Library Template:* Your soul contains an energetic template created by this journey we call life, and it arrives with you each time you take form and begin the next lifetime. It is your energetic library—your history—and it has an impact on the ways in which you engage life. This template is a part of your consciousness, carrying information about its journey across the transits of life and death through both material and immaterial realms, guiding and shaping each lifetime. This library includes a record of the energy imprints of your spiritual gift, the pathways of your core distortion, patterns you've been manifesting, and the fruits of all of your evolu-

tionary work. This library includes what some may refer to as karma, which monk and peacemaker Thich Nhat Hanh in *The Heart of the Buddha's Teaching*, describes as being a type of "volitional action" along with "formations, impulses, motivating energy ... or the will to cling to being."[4] In short, these are energy patterns that move you to act in certain ways. The record and energy pattern of this karma is associated with the energetic library of your soul matrix.

3. The Reaction Chamber: Your human body is a reaction chamber for evolving your soul. It can generate and purify the threads of light of your soul. This human body chamber process can be thought of as being like photosynthesis, which is a process in which one form of energy—sunlight—is converted into another form of energy. Just like a leaf, you absorb energies that can be transformed, in this case, into the light threads of soul. And, even one act, such as the act of invoking your spiritual gift, can affect that transformational process, creating significant changes that impact your evolution.

Your Connection to the Collective Soul Matrix: Your soul is intricately woven into the fabric of the collective light matrix of *all* souls. This field is a cosmic community of consciousness, an interwoven web of the energy waves and light beams of all souls. You are a part of this field, contributing your consciousness—and your spiritual ancestry—wherever it may be along its spiraling evolutionary path.

You are soul in a human form, and you are also simultaneously soul fused into this collective matrix. Your soul is in more than one state of being at a time—just like energy that is both waves and particles (matter). The coherent light beam of energy of your soul infuses and resides in your physical form, *while* it also is infused into the collective soul matrix, a matrix that is made of all of the soul energy matrices in creation.

Biologist Bruce Lipton summarizes an important finding of quantum physics that is instructive here when he writes in *The Biology of Belief* that "matter can simultaneously be defined as solid (particle) and as an immaterial force field (wave) ... The fact that energy and matter are one and the same is precisely what Einstein recognized ... Einstein revealed that we do not live in a universe with discrete, physical objects separated by dead space. The Universe is *one indivisible, dynamic whole* in which energy and matter are so deeply entangled it is impossible to consider them as independent elements."[5]

Your soul is an "entangled" part of this whole of creation, simultaneously infused into your human form *and* the collective soul matrix. As more people awaken to consciously evolving soul, Spirit's impulse to evolve builds exponentially in this collective matrix and ripples throughout, affecting all souls. Lipton describes the physics of the ripple effect, noting that when two pebbles of the same size are dropped from the same height at exactly the same time: "The ripples from each pebble converge on each other. Where the ripples overlap, the combined power of the interacting waves is doubled, a phenomenon referred to as constructive interference, or *harmonic resonance*."[6]

Using this description as an analogy for evolution, if you and another soul are each dropping a pebble of your conscious evolution into the collective matrix at the same time, there is a constructive effect for all. The more of us who are simultaneously, and consciously evolving, the greater the effect. We amplify each other's efforts. Your soul carries its gained wisdom—the fruits of life and evolution—into this collective field and makes it available to all.

The interdependence of the collective matrix is elegantly described in the Chinese Buddhist metaphor the Jewel Net of Indra: "Imagine a fishnet-like set of linked lines extending ad infinitum across horizontal and vertical dimensions of space. Then add more nets criss-crossing on the diagonals. Imagine an endless number of these nets criss-crossing every plane of space. At each node in every net, there is a multifaceted jewel that reflects every other jewel in the net. There is nothing outside the net and nothing that does not reverberate its presence throughout the net."[7]

There are no boundaries or barriers separating Spirit, soul, matter, and the collective soul matrix. Rather, there is a continuous luminous field of light—an always present wave eternally radiating and creating. This is the never-ending loop of the infinity symbol, creation sourcing creation. In this way all of creation evolves—evolution for the sake of evolution itself, the spark of Spirit embedded within all, manifesting creation.

When your time in your physical body comes to a close, at the death of your present human form, the energy wave of your soul will continue to be a part of the collective soul matrix, vibrating as a thread of that matrix. And when you (your soul) are called to reemerge and infuse itself into matter, "you" will once again join the cycle of being in *both* the material and the nonmaterial realms.

This occurrence can be visualized using a description that physicist David Bohm provides in *Wholeness and the Implicate Order* as an analogy for the idea of *enfolding* and *unfolding*. He describes a situation in which a drop of insoluble ink is placed in a certain type of fluid, such as glycerin, contained in two glass cylinders. There is a way in which the cylinders can be rotated such that the droplet of ink "is drawn out into a fine thread-like form that eventually becomes invisible. When the cylinder is turned in the opposite direction the thread-form draws back and suddenly becomes visible as a droplet essentially the same as the one that was there originally."[8]

Using this analogy, your soul can be thought of as being that fine thread-like form that becomes "invisible" when it leaves your physical body. Then, when creation's impulse summons the energy wave of your soul into physical manifestation, drawing the thread-form back, it will become visible in its new material form.

When your soul thus *unfolds* itself, once again simultaneously infusing its wave into a physical body and beginning a new lifetime, your entire spiritual ancestry—Spirit's creation imprint, your soul's energetic matrix, and your continuous connection to the collective matrix—will arrive with you. *"You"* includes all of your spiritual ancestry brought into this present moment of life.

My Spiritual Ancestry

When I ascended into the crystal city in that moment of receiving difficult news about my health, my heart opened, and I had the opportunity to use the components of my spiritual ancestry to further my evolution. Although I could not have articulated any specific insights in that moment, my heart instantaneously *knew* creation's blueprint within, the patterns that were calling to be transformed, and my everlasting connection to the collective of all souls.

This was a clear knowing in that timeless "moment" in the crystal city. Rumi's words convey what my heart experienced:

Hear from the heart wordless mysteries!
Understand what cannot be understood!
In man's stone-dark heart there burns a fire
That burns all veils to their root and foundation.
When the veils are burned away, the heart will
understand completely.[9]

My heart *did* understand completely. My experience revealed my knowing of the first component of spiritual ancestry: that Spirit's creation imprint is within me, and that I am carrying within me *all* of its possibilities. This realization was the beginning of a whole new sequence of evolving, of allowing, over time, the insights gained to come to the surface of my consciousness so that I could uncover and discern both the gifts and the patterns I brought with me into this lifetime—my habits and gatekeepers. Now I would learn more about these aspects of my soul's energetic matrix and library (the second component of spiritual ancestry).

It was very clear that there were deeply embedded, interconnected patterns to be consciously explored.

Next there would be the work of transforming these energies and patterns, with the help of spiritual practices. I "knew" that as a cocreator of life, a being creating with Spirit, there was in this moment enormous possibility for soul evolution, no matter what the eventual physical outcome of this manifestation referred to as MS might be. I was ecstatic as I became aware of a new edge of possibility for my soul. This joy, which some would undoubtedly find odd at such a challenging time, was vitally important. It kept me open to many possibilities, helped balance moments of fear, and kept me afloat as I learned about MS and began my healing journey. This journey has included many different emotions and stages, jolting experiences, and waves of ups and downs as I've wended my way along this unfolding pathway.

As I flashed through the "crack in the cosmic egg" and into the crystal city, remembering inner patterns to transform, I also deeply connected in a new way with my childhood journey to the portal of light and the whirling Rainbow Wheel. Later, I came to understand that connecting with the Rainbow Wheel is a way that I continually renew the Genesis Pattern within me. And I also connected, in that momentary experience, with a sense of the third component of spiritual ancestry: the collective soul matrix. The crystal fibers of the city in the heavens were woven into this collective matrix of all souls. I could "sense" these interconnections.

After my encounter with the crystal city and the whirling rainbow lights, I came away with a word (that I became aware of over time) that helped me to describe the expansive presence of this light I had been experiencing since I was five years old. That word is "Sagi" (I *feel* and *hear* the pronunciation as "say-gee-ah," and *see* it spelled as "Sagi"), which, as it turns out, is a word that is part of a phrase meaning "Great Light" or "Light of the Eyes" in ancient Aramaic and Hebrew. My understanding is that there are a few slightly different pronunciations in those languages depending on the historical period of time, but I am not certain that any of those pronunciations exactly match what I "hear." I connect with the presence of this Great Light as an access point, or portal, for the knowing of the higher consciousness of Spirit within.

Describing experiences like this, in which I suddenly know something that I wasn't aware of previously knowing, is one of those areas that Joseph Campbell refers to as being the "third best" thing in terms of describing something, since these encounters with a cosmic field of light are often beyond our ability to put into words. In fact, it actually took me a few years to bring this word, Sagi, to a conscious level. I had absorbed the energy and its information during my "moment" in the crystal city, and then waited for the insights of that journey to surface.

Over time, I have come to think of and describe this portal of the Rainbow Wheel as a field of universal Great Light. It was this Great Light and its presence that greeted me as a child, and then later it was this Great Light again that carried me into the crystal city, preparing me for the next phase of my journey of life and my unfolding evolution. It whirled me into the rainbow lights, igniting my inner strength and determination to heal, and inspiring me to evolve in as many present moments as possible.

Your Sacred Journey

As you continue to work with the four portals of the map of the Rainbow Wheel, notice the ways in which your spiritual ancestry surfaces. Connect with Spirit's creation imprint, learn more about the patterns and energies being enacted in this lifetime, and stay aware of your connection with the collective matrix. Paying conscious attention to these components of your spiritual ancestry can help facilitate your evolutionary pathway to presence—to bringing the presence of Spirit, the deep divine within, into full form as you.

And while paying attention, observing, and mindfully working toward bringing the deep divine into full form, *also* consider heeding Rumi's advice:

Don't try to figure this out.
Love's work looks absurd, but
trying to find a meaning will hide it more. Silence.[10]

Although working with the facets of your spiritual ancestry, figuring it out, *can* reveal meaning, ultimately this work—*Love's work*—may sometimes simply require silence. May this silence imbue your journey with all of the meaning that is needed for your soul to evolve.

Practices for Conscious Soul Evolution:
Your Spiritual Ancestry

Integrating Practices—practices to support embracing, anchoring, and integrating the effects of conscious soul evolution.

- **Ballooning—Taking the Ride of Your Life!**

This *Ballooning* exercise is about gaining greater awareness of energy patterns that are a part of your spiritual ancestry that may be calling to be shifted in this lifetime. You have two different types of patterns that are a part of your matrix: those that are soul-life enhancing, which you might work on amplifying and build upon for your evolution, and those that detract from your evolution, which you might consider shifting and transforming.

Taking a different view—a higher perspective—of yourself can assist you in making such a shift. In this ballooning practice you will use the art of seeing yourself from the vantage point of a higher view: a hot air balloon. If you have difficulty with heights, approach this practice of "ballooning" knowing that this particular balloon is cradled by the love of creation—swaddled in a loving embrace. Begin by closing your eyes and taking a few deep, cleansing breaths:

Now, imagine that you are climbing into the basket of a hot air balloon. The rainbow-colored balloon has been inflated and is ready to go, and your pilot is ready to take you on this open-air ascent into the sky. You lift off and begin to rise, leaving the ground and, with it, your common understandings of yourself. The air *whooshes* across your face, kissing you with the hint of new understandings. As people, houses, and cars become smaller, the sky somehow becomes larger as you shift your vision to this elevated view.

Sounds change, colors are different, and the stance of your body shifts as you gracefully glide along in the balloon, remembering that you are cradled in the love of creation. You see the crisscrossing patterns of the roadways, the meandering pathways of rivers, and a countryside dotted with pooling water. You see all of this, along with a backdrop of city buildings jutting into the sky. There are many patterns and rhythms to observe.

As you watch, you become aware that you have moved into the mode of the witness, seeing all of life without expectation or attachment to any of its patterns or possibilities. You notice an emerging realization arising that you are simply here, gently floating, suspended in beauty in this present moment, and all moments.

Along with this realization comes a sense of everything around you slowing down, and with this shift you *feel* all of you in a new way and *see* differently. You *see* yourself as the Genesis Pattern, you *know* yourself as an energy matrix made of the threads of light of creation, you *touch* your inner library—the energy record of your lifetimes, and you *sense* your connection to the collective soul matrix.

And in this slowing down and this shift of vision, you ask a question: **What energy pattern within me is calling to be shifted in this present moment?** This is a pattern that is part of your landscape, having arrived with you in this lifetime as a part of your spiritual ancestry. And now, just as you have been witnessing the patterns of the physical landscape from this higher view of the balloon, you are now asking to witness a deep inner pattern of your internal landscape. This knowing may come in words, in colors, sounds, feelings, knowings, or as an experience.

Perhaps you will see a smoky colored edge in your field that is calling to be cleared and rejuvenated through a brightly colored radiation, or you might feel a jumble of energy needing to be smoothed out, or you could hear that either a general or a specific fear is hovering. Maybe you'll simply know that humming a certain pitch will balance an energy within. Just as you have been floating in the balloon, let yourself float into this knowing of *an energy pattern within you that is calling to be shifted.*

When your time in the balloon is complete, feel it gently descend, see the landscape once again coming into closer view, feel the ever so gentle brush of the balloon touching the earth once again, and open your eyes to rejoin the view from the ground.

Spend some time recording and processing your insight—your knowing of an inner energy pattern that has come with you as part of your spiritual ancestry. Journal, walk, create art, bicycle, garden—find a way to be with the insight and to learn even more.

And then once you have furthered your conscious awareness about this pattern, *Invoke your spiritual gift or any of the fields of higher consciousness.* Invocation is a way of radiating your energetic matrix with a "constructive" wave to support you. This is a balancing wave that lends energy for shifting patterns that are calling to be transformed. So, *Invoke! And radiate yourself with the luminous, brilliant light of creation.*

Deepening Your Learning

Insights gained from exploring your spiritual ancestry contribute to bringing your presence more fully into form. Your learning can help guide your focus and intention, giving you greater clarity for discerning what is needed for your continuing evolution. The following chapter supports delving more deeply into coming to know your own presence—your divine nature within—nurturing and advancing its place in your life, for the benefit of all.

10

Presence

*Today is bright and illuminating,
illuminating, illuminating.
This love is unifying, unifying, unifying.
And it's bidding the intellect farewell,
farewell, farewell.*
—Rumi

Drawing upon the fullness of your spiritual ancestry to evolve and *be* your spiritual gift is also a process of coming to *be presence*—the fullness of the presence of Spirit, the source of creation. As you fill yourself with the radiant lights of the gifts of creation, you are coming to be the *bright, illuminating,* and *unifying* presence of divine Spirit as the sacred human being. This is a process that involves *bidding the intellect farewell*. It is through this bidding that we allow the truths of the heart—the truths of the divine self—to be revealed.

How might the experience and knowing of presence be described? What words can be used—bliss, shimmering and luminous light, ecstatic joy? Rumi is a master at using language to give you glimpses and expand your awareness of presence: he beckons you with his words. Rumi scholar and translator Andrew Harvey says in *The Way of Passion* that for Rumi the purpose of language is "to show you something far off, to show you something moving, trembling in the distance, like a heat mirage."[1] But even Rumi acknowledges the roughness of language in attempting to describe the indescribable:

Poems are rough notations for the music we are.[2]

Perhaps presence can never be fully captured with language, or distilled into explanations and ideas. After all, we are attempting to describe the divine presence of *Spirit, the Great Ultimate, God, Great Spirit, The Absolute.* Yet, there have been many poets and writers who have enticed us with their attempts.

My own words about presence are based on my direct experiences with the Rainbow Wheel, along with dreamtime encounters that have brought me new insights and understandings. Together, these understandings can be summarized as follows:

- Presence can take many different forms.
- Presence is an intense and unwavering beam of light.
- Presence illuminates a pathway for transformation.
- Presence unfolds creation's gift of possibility.

The two dreamtime experiences described next have helped me to synthesize, animate, and integrate the essence of information about presence that has come both through my direct encounters with cosmic light and through my learning from others. Conscious dreamwork can be a very powerful tool for evolution since in dreamtime you may more easily be able to go beyond your ordinary state of consciousness, bypassing cultural definitions, expectations, assumptions, and the pathways of your core distortion. Doing this allows you to access nonordinary or *extra*ordinary states of consciousness so that you may discover your deepest wisdom and the knowing of the light of creation. The Resources section at the end of the book lists a few sources that may be helpful to you in learning about conscious dreamwork.

Both of these dreamtime experiences happened while I had been intentionally attempting to gain greater understanding about the nature of "presence." RainbowHawk, an elder teacher and mentor whom I had recently met, appeared in these dreamtime sequences. RainbowHawk and his partner, WindEagle, travel the globe to offer the Earth Wisdom teachings of the *Delicate Lodge*, teachings that were brought to North America by the Mayan people. RainbowHawk and WindEagle have written about some of these teachings in their book, *Heart Seeds*, which is listed in the Resources section.

I had an opportunity to meet them at one of their book signings, after having heard about them and their work for several years. My brief introduction to them stimulated the following dreamtime experiences about "presence," which their fields of energy seemed to radiate. These dreamtime experiences helped me touch multiple dimensions of the light field of presence and to be immersed in its beauty. My previous understandings were enriched and new insights arrived. Through both of the following dreamtime sequences I was able to witness the gift of presence being offered to others.

In this first story, RainbowHawk appears in dreamtime as "Grandfather":

> My husband and I were driving Grandfather to a community gathering. It was fall, the weather was pleasant, and we were driving an older brown car. We arrived at the gathering place, which was an open expanse of land, where we were to have a picnic. Grandfather was in the backseat. We parked and then I got out, opened the door, and helped Grandfather out of the car. He was frail looking in his big bulky sweater, and he was using a tall walking stick to steady himself.
>
> As the observer of this dreamtime experience I found this very interesting because in actuality RainbowHawk, who was appearing as "Grandfather," is far from frail and is not in need of using a walking stick. Therefore, I (in my observer role) was instantly alerted to the unusual nature of this situation and wondered what RainbowHawk was up to. What was his purpose in appearing to be frail? I knew that I needed to pay close attention.
>
> We took our folding chairs out of the trunk and walked over to an area to join some other people who were already there, talking, laughing, eating, and drinking. A few beers were being consumed, but most were having nonalcoholic beverages. It was a pretty quiet group. Most of the people were between the ages of eighteen and fifty-five. Grandfather, who at eighty years of age, was clearly the elder, sat in a chair and was quiet. In fact, he did not speak at all. After a while my husband and I went over to another area and quietly talked to each other.
>
> I was keeping watch on Grandfather out of the corner of my eye, waiting. The air felt very electric and my sense was that something was going to happen soon. As the afternoon went on Grandfather seemed to be getting drunk. However, I knew that he wasn't drinking any alcohol, and in fact, my knowing was that RainbowHawk, the man playing the role of Grandfather, would not become intoxicated, so this was very uncharacteristic. Again, I wondered what RainbowHawk was doing. Why was he here incognito and why in this way? Why was he making it look as if he were intoxicated? What was his purpose?
>
> All of a sudden, from the corner of my eye, I saw Grandfather very swiftly and forcefully swing his walking stick out to his right side and whack the man sitting next to him, knocking him out of his chair. The

man was out cold on the ground. Grandfather calmly brought his walking stick back to its upright position and just stared straight ahead. Although I clearly saw him take this action there was no sound from either Grandfather or the man, and I knew there was no actual physical injury. RainbowHawk, through the use of his walking stick, moved energy in such a way that the other man was knocked over and completely incapacitated. While I was sure it was quite a jolt to the man, I knew that no harm had been done.

My husband and I just looked at each other and couldn't believe RainbowHawk (as Grandfather) had just done that. But why? What was the purpose of his action? Everyone else seemed to just ignore it. Then once again, Grandfather swiftly swung his walking stick out, this time to his left side, and whacked the other man sitting next to him. He, too, was out cold on the ground. I said to my husband that I thought it might be time to go home. I walked over to Grandfather and just played along with this drunken image he had taken on. I said aloud so that everyone around me could hear, "Okay, Grandfather, I think we'll go home now." I gently helped him to his feet, playing along with his frail and intoxicated persona, and we started walking back to the car with an unsteady and stumbling Grandfather. When we arrived at the car I opened the back door and helped him in. Then, he just slowly tipped over in the backseat, making it look as if he had just passed out.

This dreamtime sequence highlights the first core understanding that **presence can take many different forms**, and may not always be what you might expect. In fact, it might even be in a form that you *least* expect. Grandfather appeared to be an inebriated, frail, old man—harmless, of no consequence, nothing much to pay attention to. That was an illusion that he created. In actuality he was in *full presence*, more so than anyone else around him.

RainbowHawk used the illusion of inebriation in order to offer a wake-up call. This seemingly frail, elder, intoxicated man was able to knock two men out cold, flat on the ground. He was able to do this because the people at the gathering were operating under faulty assumptions, rather than being awake and paying attention to the energy around them. They weren't prepared to meet with the full force and true energy of presence. One of RainbowHawk's gifts to these men, and to the people at this gathering, was the opportunity to reflect upon how their assumptions prevented them from seeing the truth of presence.

The second core understanding, also highlighted in this dream, is that **presence is an intense and unwavering beam of light.** From watching RainbowHawk I learned about intensity in a new way. Grandfather was able to wield the intense beam of light of presence, and direct its energy toward the gift of calling his friends to wake up and join him in this field. And Grandfather was unshakable in what he was there to do. He had a mission, and there was no wavering in his energy field and his intention to call upon, in Rumi's words, the *illuminating* and *unifying* light. He used the intense light beam of presence to accomplish his mission: through the use of this steady and bright light, he was able to crack open a new possibility for these two men, and others, offering them the opportunity to see themselves and the world anew.

The field of presence is a weaving of the energy of intention and attention. RainbowHawk's clear intention to offer the field of presence, along with his impeccable attention to all of the energies present created an unwavering energy field of light in which transformation could occur. Since the two men had literally been knocked out of their current state of the ordinary mind, perhaps when they regained consciousness it would be a new consciousness in which they would immerse themselves—an awake and evolving consciousness.

The second dreamtime teaching experience deepened these understandings as well as providing new insights:

> *RainbowHawk was invited to appear on a television talk show with other Native American men and White men of European descent. He was told that the purpose was to talk about rifts in the two communities and how to work through those issues. He thought this would be okay, so he agreed to appear on the show. The twelve participating men arrived at the studio and took their seats on the stage. There were six Native American men and six White men. RainbowHawk was the elder, and all of the other men were between the ages of nineteen and fifty-five. There was a semicircle of chairs facing the direction where the audience would be; the show, however, was being taped without an audience. The host had assigned positions on the stage such that the Native American men were seated together, and the White men were seated together. RainbowHawk was sitting in the last chair in the semicircle on the right-hand side of the stage, from what would be the audience's perspective. The talk show host was a White male, about forty-five years of age.*
>
> *The show began and within a few minutes it became clear to RainbowHawk that this was actually a confrontational, attack format talk show and that the purpose was not what he had understood it to be. The talk show host was encouraging the White men to state their views and concerns in a hostile and aggressive manner. The Native American men felt energetically attacked and attempted to verbally defend themselves.*

RainbowHawk just listened for a few minutes. He very calmly discerned the situation and chose his action. All of a sudden he stood up and moved to the center of the semicircle and calmly sat on the floor with his legs crossed, his back to the men on the stage. Slowly, the other men started quieting down. The White men gave each other curious glances, as if to ask, "What is this crazy old man doing?" RainbowHawk then ever so slightly turned and made eye contact with the Native American men who then, one by one, joined him on the floor creating a circle. They intentionally left space between each other so that there was enough room for the White men to join them, if they chose to.

Softly, RainbowHawk began to chant. Then the other Native American men joined him. It was very quiet, gentle, and brief. Then there was silence. The host of the talk show stood quiet and still, and the White men also became completely silent and still. RainbowHawk spoke slowly to the circle of Native American men, saying, "I will tell you a story about my people." And then he told a story. I, as the invisible witness, did not hear the words because that did not seem to be important. What was important was the energy of the words—honoring, respectful, clear, quiet, and calm. The energy of the story was about beauty, and how hardship can be transformed into beauty.

While RainbowHawk was speaking the words of his story there was one White man who was leaning in, intently and respectfully listening. The energy was drawing him in and it was clear that he wanted to join the circle. When RainbowHawk was finished with his story it was completely quiet. Then, the man who had wanted to join the circle rose from his seat and sat on the floor in the circle in one of the spaces that had been left. He looked at RainbowHawk and said, "I will tell you a story about my people." RainbowHawk and the other Native American men gently nodded their heads, acknowledging this man, who then began to speak the words of his story.

In this dreamtime sequence, RainbowHawk again demonstrated that presence comes in many different forms. It can be subtle and quiet even though it may involve a surprising and unexpected action, like RainbowHawk sitting quietly in the middle of the stage. This was a gentle offering of radiance and an invitation for others to join this field. Or, as was demonstrated in the first dreamtime story, the form of presence can be sudden and quite startling as it offers an electrifying jolt of energy for transformational purposes.

This second story also expands on the notion that presence is an unwavering, intense beam of light. RainbowHawk was that beam of light shining upon the other men and showing them what it looks like for someone to stand in full presence and act from the unwavering light. In the face of confrontation RainbowHawk continued to walk his path in a way that was true to himself and Spirit. Not even for a moment did he allow the energy field created by the talk show host to interfere with his path of presence.

The third core understanding, that *presence illuminates a pathway for transformation*, is illustrated by both of these dreamtime encounters as well. Using presence, RainbowHawk discerned an illuminated pathway for transformation and then offered it. In the first dreamtime story an electrifying jolt of energy was needed to create the possibility for transformation. RainbowHawk rendered the energy of the ordinary into an opportunity for extraordinary transformation. In Rumi's words, RainbowHawk *bid farewell to intellect*—his actions were not what we would ordinarily consider to be logical or rational. In fact, this sudden and shocking action might be viewed as irrational, and yet it was what RainbowHawk discerned was needed in order to use himself as an instrument for illuminating a transformational pathway.

In the second dreamtime story it was a gentle gathering of energy into the circle that was needed. Again an unexpected energy was used, this time with a more gentle action, to shift confrontational energy into a peaceful gathering in such a way that it could offer healing and transformation. These two dreams demonstrated that presence illuminates a beneficial pathway given the dynamics of the present moment.

The fourth core understanding is that *presence unfolds creation's gift of possibility*. RainbowHawk demonstrated that when the *illuminating* and *unifying* light of presence shines forth, heart and imagination open and the possibilities of creation unfold. In both dreamtime stories the full energy of RainbowHawk's presence was present, and from this place he was able to offer the unfolding of all that is possible.

Your Sacred Journey

Presence is Spirit presenting itself through you, inviting you to *be many forms*, *be the intense and unwavering beam of light of you*, *be an illuminating pathway for transformation*, *be creation's unfolding gift of possibility*—***Be your Spiritual Gift!***

Philosopher and psychologist Richard Tarnas, in his book *Cosmos and Psyche*, refers to this time we live in as continuing to be dominated by the assumptions of a mechanical worldview—a view of life that has left us with a sense of meaninglessness about the cosmos and our role as humans. Tarnas, however, proposes that it is time now that we ask ourselves questions such as these:

Is it not much more plausible that human nature, in all its creative multidimensional depths and heights, emerges from the very essence of the cosmos, and that the human spirit is *the spirit of the cosmos itself* as inflected through us and enacted by us? Is it not more likely that the human intelligence in all its creative brilliance is ultimately the cosmos's intelligence expressing *its* creative brilliance? And that the human imagination is ultimately grounded in the cosmic imagination? And, finally, that this larger spirit, intelligence, and imagination all live within and act through the self-reflective human being who serves as a unique vessel and embodiment of the cosmos—creative, unpredictable, fallible, self-transcending, unfolding the whole, integral to the whole, perhaps even essential to the whole?[3]

To these questions I answer *Yes!* We are the Spirit—*the Presence*—of the cosmos, of creation itself, essential to the whole, and grounded in the infinite possibility of creation's brilliance.

Over time, as I have practiced invocation and explored the essence of presence, I have come to a place in which I am able to speak the words "I *am* Peace" and know the truth of the vibration of these words. And further, I am also able to stand in the center of my soul's knowing and say, *"I Am,"* knowing that this "am-ness" is the presence of Spirit in the form of me: the *Sacred Human Being*, unfolding creation.

As you practice and explore, *May you know that you are your spiritual gift and the Presence of Spirit.*

Practices for Conscious Soul Evolution: The Rainbow Wheel Ceremony

Integrating Practices—practices to support embracing, anchoring, and integrating the effects of conscious soul evolution.

• A Ceremony of Presence

Ceremonies are ways of calling forth, enlivening, and immersing ourselves in particular energies. You have experienced many types of ceremonies throughout the course of your life—birthday celebrations, weddings and commitment ceremonies, baptisms, rituals for naming babies, and funerals. You may have participated in prayer offerings in which candles are lit, the fragrance and beauty of flowers fill the space, or incense or sage is burned.

The world's spiritual traditions are rich in their ways of creating sacred space and holding ceremony. And ceremony can also be created by any given individual: *you* can create a sacred space and conduct a ceremony for the purpose of your evolution. The Rainbow Wheel Ceremony supports you in invoking each of the thirteen gifts of this wheel, and focusing your attention on summoning forth the energy of each of these fields of higher consciousness. With this ceremony you are building your skill and increasing your capacity for focused attention, which will affect the spiraling path of your soul evolution and the radiance of your presence here in the form of the sacred human being. Attention is key for evolution. The instructions for this Rainbow Wheel Ceremony follow:

Step 1: This is a ceremony that you will conduct over a period of thirteen days. You might decide to do this in thirteen consecutive days, or in three smaller pieces. You can think of this as either one long intensive or three shorter intensives. Each day you will be focusing your attention throughout the day on a particular spiritual gift. In addition, you'll need to set aside about an hour to focus specifically on the gift for that day, although for part of that time you might also be engaged in another activity such as taking a walk or working in the garden. What is important here is engaging in an activity that will support your attention to the gift.

Discern for yourself—for the structure of your life—which form, the longer intensive or the three shorter intensives, will work better. Conducting this ceremony across thirteen days without interruption helps sustain the energetic field for the ceremony, building momentum as you go. For some, however, the three shorter intensives might be a preferable method since it allows for brief periods of integration.

If you choose to do the three shorter intensives (five days, four days, and then four days again), I suggest that you do not separate them by more than a week, so that you can more readily build on the momentum of the previous segment. You might also consider doing a journaling practice or find some other way of consciously processing each segment you've just completed. This will also help bridge across the shorter intensive periods.

Each of the thirteen days of the ceremony you will begin by discerning which gift to focus on that day. Begin the first day of the ceremony as follows:

Find a quiet place that feels relaxing to you, and in that space sit quietly, with your eyes closed, gently breathing. When your breath is relaxed and you feel its energy flowing easefully throughout, offer your gratitude to all of creation and see that you are connecting to the life-force energy of the earth and all of the cosmos. Next, using your higher inner vision, see the radiant, rainbow lights of creation above you. This may be a luminous whirling wheel, or perhaps streaks of brilliant light. Then ask:

Which gift of higher consciousness am I to focus on today for the benefit of all?

You may hear a response, you might have a feeling or sensation that informs you, or you might just *know* it. It could come to you immediately, or it might take several minutes. If you don't have a sense of a particular gift to focus on, simply pick any one of the gifts to begin with. Once you know the gift, invoke that field of higher consciousness to fill all of you. Then open your eyes, write in your journal the gift of the day to focus on, and begin your day.

Step 2: As you move through your day, pause and invoke this gift, each time filling all of you—your body and soul—with the energy wave of this gift. Do this many times throughout the day. Also notice how this gift affects you, what happens throughout your day that may be different, or perhaps is related to this gift in some way. Take note of questions you might be having, or what you find yourself drawn to think about or ponder. At some point during the day, take about an hour to specifically focus on this gift. Ask this question during this time and see what comes to you:

What is needed for my evolution with this gift of ... (speak the name of the gift)?

Once you've asked this question, you might take a walk, journal, garden, create some form of art or music, or meditate. What is important is creating a space for yourself to *be*, and allowing yourself to know what is needed. There are many different types of responses you might find coming into your awareness. It might seem directly related, or it might not. Trust the process and allow yourself space for exploration. I also suggest some form of journaling to help focus your attention, and to track the wisdom that unfolds for you.

When I asked this question about what is needed for my evolution with the gift of *Joy*, I saw, with my higher vision, a bright light and knew that I needed to focus my attention on the many forms of "brightness." I had asked this question at the start of a walk and so while walking I intentionally looked for "brightness" and noticed how it made me feel. I experienced brightness when a neighbor's dog greeted me enthusiastically, when a bright red cardinal sang its song, when the sun's light danced through the leaves, and when my young neighbor got off the school bus, picked a flower, and, with much brightness in her step and in her smile, ran over to me and gave me the flower. I *felt* joy. And I spent the rest of the day basking in its brightness, knowing that evolving *Joy*, for me, has to do with seeing brightness in its many forms.

If sometime after you've asked the question about what is needed and you feel that you are just not tapping into a stream of knowing about this, you might use *The Clear Light of the Heart Meditation* to take yourself into a deeper dimension, and then ask again.

Also as part of the process pay attention to your dreams. If you remember anything about your dreams upon awakening, record them and see if they bring new insights and understandings.

Step 3: Each day upon arising, take a few deep breaths to bring yourself into the present moment, and then ask:

> *Of the remaining gifts, what is the gift for me to focus on today for the benefit of all?*
> (You might want to keep a list of the gifts you've focused on and which you have remaining in order to help guide you each day.)

Once you've identified the gift, invoke it and then begin your day going through the same process described in **Step 2,** for each of the thirteen days. Throughout the day remember to invoke the gift for that day, often.

Step 4: Toward evening of the last day of this ceremony, once again sit in silence and breathe easefully. Close your eyes and with your higher vision see all of the rainbow lights of creation. Offer your gratitude, breathe in the energies of these lights, and know that these energies of creation walk with you on each step of your journey as soul, here on earth, in this present moment as the sacred human *being.*

Expanding Possibilities

Presence is expansive—it is sourced by the infinite possibilities of creation. All of your evolutionary work now takes you to the next turn in the spiral of your unfolding pathway. You *are* the shimmering rainbow lights of creation, containing *all* of the spiritual gifts of this luminous, brilliant light.

11
The Shimmering Rainbow Lights of Creation

The Rainbow Wheel has seeped into my consciousness. My learning has come in varying forms and in different ways, with the journey having had many different types of moments—gentle, startling, joyful, frightening, blissful, challenging, and blessed. In the past several years I have been able to reflect and see some of the larger patterns, deriving the golden nuggets from a wide range of pieces of information and experiences. However, one piece of information, in particular, has been crystal clear for many years: knowing that **we all have a spiritual gift that is a key to opening new gateways for soul evolution.**

In the Introduction, I told the story of my dreamtime voyage to the source of light that conveyed a vision of my work for this lifetime, and what I later came to know as the Rainbow Wheel map for conscious soul evolution. As I've opened the packets of energy and information about the Rainbow Wheel from the portal of cosmic light, extraordinary experiences have tumbled onto my path. I've opened to seeing and touching more of life, and life has responded.

Ralph Metzner, in *The Unfolding Self*, writes, "This world has been transformed, if our journey has been successful, into a new world seen with fresh eyes. The end of the journey is the beginning of a new, empowered way of life."[1] My *conscious* journey of seeing with "fresh eyes" began after my encounter in the crystal city, which I described in Chapter 9. There, after joyfully merging with the rainbow lights of creation, I returned to this dimension of physical life knowing that everything had changed and that *life* was just beginning.

There have been many phases to this new life, numerous starts and stops, and various challenges along the way while discerning the pathway to follow. There have been difficult life circumstances with which to contend, and also much radiance and joy. While there has been plenty of grist for the mill of transformation, it all has been a gift of the highest order and I embrace this continuing, unfolding journey of creating life. There have been incredible synchronicities, amazing guidance offered, and many blessings. I am grateful for all of it.

In the dreamtime sequence presented in Chapter 10, RainbowHawk told a story of his people transforming hardship into beauty. I believe that many of us, perhaps all, carry such individual stories of hardship, and we also tap into the collective soul matrix knowing of such stories. What I have gleaned from my journey is that we additionally have the ability to tap into the stories of beauty—to see life from the higher and more expansive view of the whirling rainbow lights of creation.

From this view of higher consciousness we can see new pathways for transforming hardship into beauty, and difficult and challenging life moments into deeper understanding. We can seize the moment for the purpose of transformation: we can receive light, information, energy, and inspiration for consciously remembering our divine nature, and for evolving our souls.

An Invitation

The final offering of this book is an invitation to step, even more deeply, into the full resonance of the whirling rainbow lights of creation. I invite you to merge with this whirling field of light, infusing yourself with the incredible view from this field of higher consciousness. You can use the following meditation to immerse yourself and merge with the rainbow lights. Know that at any time in your life you can take this higher perspective, seeing the possibilities you might unfold. *May this view from higher consciousness, this whirling energy of life, be a blessing.*

Here are the instructions for the *Shimmering Rainbow Lights of Creation* meditation (an audio file of this meditation is available at the author's website, www.joelise.com):

Begin by lying on your back or sitting in a comfortably supported position. Close your eyes and breathe deeply to clear yourself. Breathe in through your nose and release the breath out through your mouth, cleansing yourself of all tension being held at the moment. Breathe easily and deeply, filling yourself fully with your breath—filling your lungs and your abdominal area. As you release the breath, release any tension and stress you have been holding. Take a full breath in through your nose, and release the breath out through your mouth. And when you are ready, bring your breath to a gentle and rhythmic state, changing the breath pattern to gently inhaling through your nose, and also gently exhaling through your nose. Continue to feel your body filling with the breath, your belly and chest expanding and releasing with each cycle of the breath.

Now, put your right palm on your heart. Gently breathe into your heart. See the breath flow into all of the chambers of your heart, and as you breathe see that the breath is made of pure, clear light. Feel the light filling all of the chambers of your heart, and as it does so, see your heart opening like a beautiful flower coming into full bloom. Know that you are in the center of the clear light of creation. With each breath see the light filling every fiber of your physical body and your energetic field. Also see the light moving out beyond you, filling all of the space around you with this luminous, brilliant light of creation.

Offer your gratitude for the love of this light and then send the light above and below for the benefit of All. With the inbreath, fill all of yourself with the light. With the outbreath, see the light flowing out of you to all of creation. It is moving out the top of your head—your crown chakra—to the sky, and it is flowing out the bottoms of your feet to the earth. With each complete cycle of the breath, the light fills all of you and all of creation.

Now, focus your breath on the heart, breathing the light into your heart. And as you gently and easefully breathe, see that above you there is a whirling, luminous, radiant field of rainbow lights. This glowing field may be silent, or you may hear a vibration or tone coming from the lights. Allow yourself to rise up into the rainbow lights. As you enter this field, open your heart space to receiving the energy of this consciousness, this light of creation. Breathe this energy into your heart, feeling your heart space opening and receiving this light. Sense the energy and know the presence of this field. Delight in the wonders of the rainbow lights of creation.

Immerse yourself in this field. Breathe in its radiance, and wisdom, while breathing out and releasing back into the void anything that interferes with the knowing of your oneness with this field and all of creation. Allow yourself to *be* one with the shimmering, whirling rainbow lights. See, sense, feel, and know yourself and all of creation from this higher view of life. Open to exploring life from this higher view. See and know yourself from this field of higher consciousness. You *are* all of the spiritual gifts of creation. You *are* the rainbow lights. Truly allow yourself to *be* in this field.

Then, whenever you are ready, bring yourself and all of the rainbow lights fully into this dimension and your physical body. See yourself standing on the earth, grounded, here and now, as a being of the rainbow lights. And when you are ready, open your eyes with the knowing that **You are a Celebration of Light and Life—a Celebration of Soul!**

The treasure of gifts has arrived.
The brilliance of the sea has flashed forth.
The dawn of blessing has arisen.[2]
       —Rumi

GLOSSARY

The story of the Rainbow Wheel uses my emerging understandings of certain words—Spirit, consciousness, soul, conscious evolution, energy, matter, unfolding, and collective soul matrix. These words and their meanings are a significant part of a global conversation that is occurring. There are many questions we might explore about these words: What is the shared meaning for these words? What are our different understandings? What are the stories we are telling about our knowings of these words and the energies they hold?

The global conversation is being spun and woven from such questions. Stories, both old and new, of many kinds are emerging—personal, experiential, researched, ancient, tribal, cultural, religious, scientific, psychological, and mythic stories. We are learning and we are creating. We are dialoguing.

Through our explorations, conversations, and the sharing of our stories we are creating a context for the usage of these words. As philosopher Ken Wilber writes in *The Eye of Spirit*, "We exist in fields within fields, patterns within patterns, contexts within contexts, endlessly."[1] Speaking our stories, whether they are our scientifically researched stories or our personal stories, allows us to see some of the patterns and contexts. If we clarify our meanings for ourselves and each other, we can come to a deeper understanding, collectively.

I'd like to briefly describe how I am using these words—Spirit, consciousness, soul, conscious evolution, energy, matter, unfolding, and collective soul matrix—in relationship to the Rainbow Wheel story. And as you work with the Rainbow Wheel, I invite you into the center of your own current understandings, while also opening to new possibilities. We are poised at a new frontier of knowing as we weave our collective tapestry, a rich fabric of radiant, luminous threads of knowing.

Spirit

Spirit is the source of creation, of all that is. It permeates all. It *is* the void, the plenum, the ground field. It is consciousness. *It is all.*

Consciousness

This term derives from the Latin word meaning "what is known all together."[2] "Known" as I use it here encompasses body, heart, Spirit, and soul. So, for example, my consciousness includes what is "known" from the direct, ecstatic experiences I've had with the luminous portal of light. My consciousness contains everything I "know" from my stage of development or evolution. And since all consciousness throughout creation is connected, *I* also contain within me the essence of the consciousness of all of creation. This "knowing" resides in our deepest inner territories—in our cells and in the essence of our beings.

Soul

Soul is the light and consciousness of Spirit fused, through the cycles of life and death, into a coherent beam of light—like a laser beam. The light and consciousness of Spirit manifest into the light and consciousness of soul. As we make our way through these cycles, the light of soul is purified and rarefied, much like the process of a grain of sand being turned into a pearl—a pearl that is individuated and yet connected to and containing the imprint of *all* of the essence of Spirit.

Conscious Evolution

Conscious evolution is the intentional choice to evolve soul—to direct our intention and attention to this endeavor. What this means for me is that I choose: I actively *intend* to evolve soul, and I *attend* to this endeavor by engaging in spiritual and life practices that support this choice and intention.

Energy

The cosmos is an ocean of energy arising from the "void" of creation. It is the moving, vital force behind all of existence.

Matter

The energetic ocean of the cosmos is brimming with particles of life—wondrous "bits of matter"[3] that come together, cohering into infinite forms that we refer to as the "physical" or "material." And that matter is made of energy, the same energy of Spirit.

Unfolding

The field that contains all of the potential of creation—the existence of everything—has commonly been referred to as "the void," the "plenum," and "the ground field." Matter and all of life "unfold" from this field. For example, I can say that I have been continually unfolding my life and my evolution from the ground field, the void, of all that is.

Collective Soul Matrix

Each soul is part of a collective of all souls. This is a field of all souls woven into a matrix, an array of souls all connected and part of one field of light and consciousness. Being connected to this field is a way in which the evolution of my soul affects you and the evolution of your soul.

CHAPTER NOTES

Preface

1. Coleman Barks, *The Soul of Rumi: A New Collection of Ecstatic Poems* (San Francisco: HarperCollins, 2001), p. 345.

2. Christina Baldwin, *Storycatcher: Making Sense of Our Lives through the Power and Practice of Story* (Novato, CA: New World Library, 2005), p. 224.

Chapter 1. Light Journeys

1. Joseph Chilton Pearce, *The Crack in the Cosmic Egg: New Constructs of Mind and Reality* (Rochester, VT: Park Street Press, 2002), p. xiv.

2. Ervin Laszlo, *Science and the Akashic Field: An Integral Theory of Everything* (Rochester, VT: Inner Traditions, 2004), p. 155.

3. Russell Targ, *Limitless Mind: A Guide to Remote Viewing and Transformation of Consciousness* (Novato, CA: New World Library, 2004), p. xvii.

4. Andrew Harvey, *The Way of Passion: A Celebration of Rumi* (Berkeley, CA: Frog, 1994), p. 219.

5. Dean Radin, *Entangled Minds: Extrasensory Experiences in a Quantum Reality* (New York: Paraview Pocket Books, 2006), p. 14.

6. Coleman Barks, *The Soul of Rumi: A New Collection of Ecstatic Poems* (San Francisco: HarperCollins, 2001), p. 56.

7. Ibid., p. 14

Chapter 2. The Story of the Rainbow Wheel

1. Ralph Metzner, *The Unfolding Self: Varieties of Transformative Experience* (Novato, CA: Origin Press, 1998), p. 2.

2. Ibid., p. 1.

3. Ibid.

4. Ken Wilber, "A Spirituality That Transforms," *What Is Enlightenment?* 12 (1997): 23–32.

5. Metzner, *The Unfolding Self*, p. 233.

6. Roger Walsh, *Essential Spirituality: The 7 Central Practices to Awaken Heart and Mind* (New York: John Wiley & Sons, 1999), p. 7.

7. Christopher M. Bache, *Dark Night, Early Dawn: Steps to a Deep Ecology of Mind* (Albany: State University of New York Press, 2000), p. 230.

8. Allan Combs, *The Radiance of Being: Understanding the Grand Integral Vision; Living the Integral Life* (St. Paul, MN: Paragon House), p. 285.

9. Coleman Barks, *The Soul of Rumi: A New Collection of Ecstatic Poems* (San Francisco: HarperCollins, 2001), p. 235.

10. Ibid., p. 144.

11. Ibid., p. 4.

12. Ibid.

13. Ibid., p. 260.

14. Ken Wilber, *Integral Spirituality: A Startling New Role for Religion in the Modern and Postmodern World* (Boston: Integral Books, 2006), p. 203.

15. Christina Baldwin, *Storycatcher: Making Sense of Our Lives through the Power and Practice of Story* (Novato, CA: New World Library, 2005), p. 27.

16. Ibid., p. 31.

17. Ibid., p. 20.

Chapter 3. A Map for Conscious Soul Evolution

1. Drunvalo Melchizedek, The Ancient Secret of the Flower of Life, vol. 1 (Flagstaff, AZ: Light Technology Publlishing, 1998), p. 171.

2. Coleman Barks, *The Soul of Rumi: A New Collection of Ecstatic Poems* (San Francisco: HarperCollins, 2001), p. 18.

3. Coleman Barks, *The Soul of Rumi: A New Collection of Ecstatic Poems* (San Francisco: HarperCollins, 2001), p. 255.

4. Ken Wilber, *Integral Spirituality: A Startling New Role for Religion in the Modern and Postmodern World* (Boston: Integral Books, 2006), p. 125.

5. Shahram Shiva, *Hush, Don't Say Anything to God: Passionate Poems of Rumi* (Fremont, CA: Jain Publishing, 2000), p. 96.

6. Coleman Barks, *The Soul of Rumi: A New Collection of Ecstatic Poems* (San Francisco: HarperCollins, 2001), p. 38.

Chapter 4. Identifying Your Spiritual Gift

1. Julia Cameron, *The Right to Write* (New York: Jeremy P. Tarcher/Putnam, 1998), p. xvi.

2. Christina Baldwin, *Storycatcher: Making Sense of Our Lives through the Power and Practice of Story* (Novato, CA: New World Library, 2005), p. 40.

3. Michael Talbot, *The Holographic Universe* (New York: HarperPerennial, 1991), pp. 164–65.

4. Andrew Harvey, *The Way of Passion: A Celebration of Rumi* (Berkeley, CA: Frog, 1994), p. 51.

Chapter 5. Portal One: Invoking Your Spiritual Gift

1. Christina Baldwin, *Seven Whispers: Listening to the Voice of Spirit* (Novato, CA: New World Library, 2002), p. 1.

2. Andrew Harvey, *The Way of Passion: A Celebration of Rumi* (Berkeley, CA: Frog, 1994), p. 123.

3. Allan Combs, *The Radiance of Being: Understanding the Grand Integral Vision; Living the Integral Life* (St. Paul, MN: Paragon House), p. 247.

4. Andrew Cohen and Ken Wilber, "Following the Grain of the Kosmos," *What Is Enlightenment?* 25 (2004): 45–52.

5. Ralph Metzner, *The Unfolding Self: Varieties of Transformative Experience* (Novato, CA: Origin Press, 1998), p. 176.

6. José Argüelles, *The Mayan Factor: Path Beyond Technology* (Rochester, VT: Bear, 1987), p. 54.

7. Russell Targ, *Limitless Mind: A Guide to Remote Viewing and Transformation of Consciousness* (Novato, CA: New World Library, 2004), p. xvii.

8. Masaru Emoto, *The True Power of Water: Healing and Discovering Ourselves* (Hillsboro, OR: Beyond Words, 2005), p. 12.

9. Combs, *The Radiance of Being*, p. 165.

10. Harvey, *The Way of Passion*, p. 130.

11. Shahram Shiva, *Hush, Don't Say Anything to God: Passionate Poems of Rumi* (Fremont, CA: Jain Publishing, 2000), p. 121.

12. Ibid., p. 122.

13. Lama Surya Das, *Awakening the Buddha Within: Tibetan Wisdom for the Western World* (New York: Broadway Books, 1997), pp. 262–63.

14. Ibid., p. 301.

15. Ibid., p. 343.

16. Jill Kimberly Hartwell Geoffrion, *Praying the Labyrinth* (Cleveland, OH: Pilgrim Press, 1999), p. vii.

17. Ibid., p. xi.

18. Harvey, *The Way of Passion*, p. 110.

19. Ibid., p. 132.

20. Christina Baldwin, *Calling the Circle: The First and Future Culture* (Newberg, OR: SwanRaven, 1994), p. 24.

Chapter 6. Portal Two: Liberating the Gatekeepers

1. Robert Fritz, *The Path of Least Resistance: Learning to Become the Creative Force in Your Own Life* (New York: Fawcett Columbine, 1984), p. 3.

2. Ralph Metzner, *The Unfolding Self: Varieties of Transformative Experience* (Novato, CA: Origin Press, 1998), p. 36.

3. David R. Hawkins, *Power vs. Force: The Hidden Determinants of Human Behavior* (Sedona, AZ: Veritas, 1998), p. 32.

4. Brian Swimme and Thomas Berry, *The Universe Story: From the Primordial Flaring Forth to the Ecozoic Era—A Celebration of the Unfolding of the Cosmos* (San Francisco: HarperCollins, 1992), p. 53.

5. Shahram Shiva, *Hush, Don't Say Anything to God: Passionate Poems of Rumi* (Fremont, CA: Jain Publishing, 2000), p. 11.

6. Coleman Barks, *The Soul of Rumi: A New Collection of Ecstatic Poems* (San Francisco: HarperCollins, 2001), p. 21.

7. Ibid., p. 168.

8. Bruce Lipton, *The Biology of Belief: Unleasing the Power of Consciousness, Matter, and Miracles* (Santa Rosa, CA: Mountain of Love/Elite Books, 2005), pp. 49–50.

Chapter 7. Portal Three: Spiraling Breath

1. Ralph Metzner, *The Unfolding Self: Varieties of Transformative Experience* (Novato, CA: Origin Press, 1998) p. 112.

2. Peter Senge, C. Otto Scharmer, Joseph Jaworski, and Betty Sue Flowers, *Presence: Human Purpose and the Field of the Future* (Cambridge, MA: Society for Organizational Learning, 2004), p. 72.

3. Coleman Barks, *The Soul of Rumi: A New Collection of Ecstatic Poems* (San Francisco: HarperCollins, 2001), p. 127.

Chapter 8. Portal Four: Renewing the Genesis Pattern

1. Coleman Barks, *The Soul of Rumi: A New Collection of Ecstatic Poems* (San Francisco: HarperCollins, 2001), p. 371.

2. Ibid., p. 263.

3. Shahram Shiva, *Hush, Don't Say Anything to God: Passionate Poems of Rumi* (Fremont, CA: Jain Publishing, 2000), p. 31.

Chapter 9. Your Spiritual Ancestry

1. Coleman Barks, *The Soul of Rumi: A New Collection of Ecstatic Poems* (San Francisco: HarperCollins, 2001), p. 179.

2. Joseph Campbell with Bill Moyers, *The Power of Myth* (New York: Anchor Books, 1991), p. 58. Campbell is referring to the eighteenth-century German philosopher Immanuel Kant (1724–1804).

3. Brian Swimme and Thomas Berry, *The Universe Story: From the Primordial Flaring Forth to the Ecozoic Era—A Celebration of the Unfolding of the Cosmos* (San Francisco: HarperSanFrancisco), p. 17.

4. Thich Nhat Hanh, *The Heart of the Buddha's Teaching: Transforming Suffering into Peace, Joy, and Liberation* (New York: Broadway Books, 1998), p. 227.

5. Bruce Lipton, *The Biology of Belief: Unleashing the Power of Consciousness, Matter, and Miracles* (Santa Rosa, CA: Mountain of Love/Elite Books, 2005), p. 102.

6. Ibid., p. 116.

7. Stephanie Kaza, "First Do No Harm," *Shambhala Sun*, March 2007, p. 42.

8. David Bohm, *Wholeness and the Implicate Order* (New York: ARK Paperbacks, 1983), p. 179.

9. Andrew Harvey, *The Way of Passion: A Celebration of Rumi* (Berkeley, CA: Frog, 1994), p. 164.

10. Barks, *The Soul of Rumi*, p. 26.

Chapter 10. Presence

1. Andrew Harvey, *The Way of Passion: A Celebration of Rumi* (Berkeley, CA: Frog, 1994), p. 120.

2. Coleman Barks, *The Soul of Rumi: A New Collection of Ecstatic Poems* (San Francisco: HarperCollins, 2001), p. 134.

3. Richard Tarnas, *Cosmos and Psyche: Intimations of a New World View* (New York: Viking, 2006), p. 492.

Chapter 11. The Shimmering Rainbow Lights of Creation

1. Ralph Metzner, *The Unfolding Self: Varieties of Transformative Experience* (Novato, CA: Origin Press, 1998), p. 226.

2. Coleman Barks, *The Soul of Rumi: A New Collection of Ecstatic Poems* (San Francisco: HarperCollins, 2001), p. 316.

Glossary

1. Ken Wilber, *The Eye of Spirit: An Integral Vision for a World Gone Slightly Mad* (Boston: Shambhala, 2001), p. 90.

2. David Bohm and F. David Peat, *Science, Order, and Creativity* (New York: Routledge, 2000), p. 212.

3. Brian Swimme and Thomas Berry, *The Universe Story: From the Primordial Flaring Forth to the Ecozoic Era—A Celebration of the Unfolding of the Cosmos* (San Francisco: HarperSanFrancisco, 1992), p. 280.

RESOURCES

There are many resources in the form of books, articles, CDs, DVDs, and Web sites available to support you in your evolutionary journey. What follows are a few resources that you may find helpful, specifically in relation to the Rainbow Wheel. Some of these resources are direct in their application, and others provide background or related information. (Note that items with an asterisk offer suggestions and directions for practices, meditations, ceremonies, and exercises to support you in your conscious soul evolution. While some of the other resources listed also make note of practices you might embrace, those with an asterisk offer a series of specific instructions.)

Conscious Evolution

*Ardagh, Arjuna. *The Translucent Revolution: How People Just Like You Are Waking Up and Changing the World.* Novato, CA: New World Library, 2005.

Argüelles, José. *The Mayan Factor: Path Beyond Technology.* Rochester, VT: Bear, 1987.

Beck, Donald, and Cowan, Christopher C. *Spiral Dynamics: Mastering Values, Leadership, and Change.* Malden, MA: Blackwell, 1996.

Bache, Christopher M. *Dark Night, Early Dawn: Steps to a Deep Ecology of Mind.* Albany: State University of New York Press, 2000.

*Baldwin, Christina. *The Seven Whispers: Listening to the Voice of Spirit.* Novato, CA: New World Library, 2002.

Calleman, Carl Johan. *The Mayan Calendar and the Transformation of Consciousness.* Rochester, VT: Bear, 2004.

Coelho, Paulo. *The Alchemist.* San Francisco: HarperCollins, 1993.

Combs, Allan. *The Radiance of Being: Understanding the Grand Integral Vision; Living the Integral Life.* St. Paul, MN: Paragon House, 2002.

Emoto, Masaru. *The Hidden Messages in Water.* Hillsboro, OR: Beyond Words Publishing, 2004.

Emoto, Masaru. *The True Power of Water: Healing and Discovering Ourselves.* Hillsboro, OR: Beyond Words Publishing, 2005.

Evolve: www.evolve.org.

*Gawain, Shaktii. *Living in the Light: A Guide to Personal and Planetary Transformation.* Novato, CA: New World Library, 1998.

*Gawain, Shaktii. *The Path of Transformation: How Healing Ourselves Can Change the World.* Novato, CA: New World Library, 2000.

Goswami, Amit. *Physics of the Soul: The Quantum Book of Living, Dying, Reincarnation, and Immortality.* Charlottesville, VA: Hampton Roads, 2001.

Harvey, Andrew. *The Way of Passion: A Celebration of Rumi.* Berkeley, CA: Frog, 1994.

Hawkins, David R. *Power vs. Force: The Hidden Determinants of Human Behavior.* Sedona, AZ: Veritas, 1998.

Hillman, Anne. *The Dancing Animal Woman.* Norfolk, CT: Bramble Books, 1994.

Institute of Noetic Sciences: www.noetic.org.

Integral Institute: www.integralinstitute.org.

Kyabgon, Traleg. *The Essence of Buddhism: An Introduction to Its Philosophy and Practice.* Boston: Shambhala, 2001.

Laszlo, Ervin. *Science and the Akashic Field: An Integral Theory of Everything.* Rochester, VT: Inner Traditions, 2004.

Metzner, Ralph. *The Unfolding Self: Varieties of Transformative Experience*. Novato, CA: Origin Press, 1998.

*Mossbridge, Julia. *Unfolding: The Perpetual Science of Your Soul's Work*. Novato, CA: New World Library, 2002.

*Myss, Caroline. *Entering the Castle: An Inner Path to God and Your Soul*. New York: Free Press, 2007.

New Dimensions Media: www.newdimensions.org.

Pearce, Joseph Chilton. *The Biology of Transcendence: A Blueprint of the Human Spirit*. Rochester, VT: Park Street Press, 2002.

Pearce, Joseph Chilton. *The Crack in the Cosmic Egg: New Constructs of Mind and Reality*. Rochester, VT: Park Street Press, 2002.

Swimme, Brian, and Berry, Thomas. *The Universe Story: From the Primordial Flaring Forth to the Ecozoic Era—A Celebration of the Unfolding of the Cosmos*. San Francisco: HarperCollins, 1992.

Targ, Russell. *Limitless Mind: A Guide to Remote Viewing and Transformation of Consciousness*. Novato, CA: New World Library, 2004.

Wilber, Ken. *Integral Spirituality: A Startling New Role for Religion in the Modern and Postmodern World*. Boston: Integral Books, 2006.

Wilber, Ken. *A Theory of Everything: An Integral Vision for Business, Politics, Science and Spirituality*. Boston: Shambhala, 2001.

Invocation and Sacred Space

*Andrews, Lynn V. *Teachings around the Sacred Wheel: Finding the Soul of the Dreamtime*. San Francisco: HaperCollins, 1990.

*Andrews, Ted. *Animal Speak: The Spiritual and Magical Powers of Creatures Great and Small*. St. Paul, MN: Llewellyn Publications, 2003.

*Douglas-Klotz, Neil. *Blessings of the Cosmos: Wisdom of the Heart from the Aramaic Words of Jesus*. Boulder, CO: Sounds True, 2006.

*Douglas-Klotz, Neil. *The Hidden Gospel: Decoding the Spiritual Message of the Aramaic Jesus*. Wheaton, IL: Quest Books, 1999.

*Meadows, Kenneth. *Shamanic Spirit: A Practical Guide to Personal Fulfillment*. Rochester, VT: Bear, 2004.

*Melchizedek, Drunvalo. *Living in the Heart: How to Enter into the Sacred Space within the Heart*. Flagstaff, AZ: Light Technology Publishing, 2003.

McCraty, Rollin. "The Resonant Heart." *Shift: At the Frontiers of Consciousness* 5 (Dec. 2004–Feb. 2005): 15–19.

Sams, Jamie. *The 13 Original Clan Mothers: Your Sacred Path to Discovering the Gifts, Talents & Abilities of the Feminine through the Ancient Teachings of the Sisterhood*. San Francisco: HarperCollins, 1993.

Sacred Geometry

Melchizedek, Drunvalo. *The Ancient Secret of the Flower of Life*, vol. 1. Flagstaff, AZ: Light Technology Publishing, 1998.

Melchizedek, Drunvalo. *The Ancient Secret of the Flower of Life*, vol. 2. Flagstaff, AZ: Light Technology Publishing, 2000.

Lawlor, Robert. *Sacred Geometry: Philosophy and Practice*. New York: Thames & Hudson, 1982.

Schneider, Michael S. *A Beginner's Guide to Constructing the Universe: The Mathematical Archetypes of Nature, Art and Science—A Voyage from 1 to 10*. New York: Harper Collins, 1994.

www.spiraloflight.com

Meditation and Breathwork

*Hendricks, Gay. *Conscious Breathing: Breathwork for Health, Stress Release, and Personal Mastery.* New York: Bantam, 1995.

* Khalsa, Dharma Singh, and Stauth, Cameron. *Meditation as Medicine: Activate the Power of Your Natural Healing Force.* New York: Fireside, 2002.

*Lama Surya Das. *Awakening the Buddha Within: Tibetan Wisdom for the Western World.* New York: Broadway Books, 1997.

*Swami Durgananda. *The Heart of Meditation: Pathways to a Deeper Experience.* South Fallsburg, NY: Siddha Yoga Publications, 2002.

*Wallace, B. Allan. *The Attention Revolution: Unlocking the Power of the Focused Mind.* Boston: Wisdom Publications, 2006.

*Weiss, Andrew. *Beginning Mindfulness: Learning the Way of Awareness.* Novato, CA: New World Library, 2004.

*Wilber, Ken. *The Eye of Spirit: An Integral Vision for a World Gone Slightly Mad.* Boston: Shambhala, 2001 (pages 295–303 provide a guide for meditation).

The Labyrinth

*Hartwell Geoffrion, Jill Kimberly. *Living the Labyrinth.* Cleveland, OH: Pilgrim Press, 2000.

*Hartwell Geoffrion, Jill Kimberly. *Praying the Labyrinth.* Cleveland, OH: Pilgrim Press, 1994.

Labyrinth Society, www.labyrinthsociety

Purce, Jill. *The Mystic Spiral: Journey of the Soul.* New York: Thames and Hudson, 1974.

The Medicine Wheel

*Meadows, Kenneth. *Earth Medicine: A Shamanic Way to Self Discovery*. Rockport, MA: Element, 1989.

*Meadows, Kenneth. *The Medicine Way: A Shamanic Path to Self Discovery*. Rockport, MA: Element, 1990.

McGaa, Ed (Eagle Man). *Mother Earth Spirituality: Native American Paths to Healing Ourselves and Our World*. New York: HarperCollins, 1990.

McGaa, Ed (Eagle Man). *Rainbow Tribe: Ordinary People Journeying on the Red Road*. New York: HarperCollins, 1992.

Storm, Hyemeyohsts. *Lightningbolt*. New York: Ballantine, 1994.

WhiteEagle, www.dancehammers.org.

WindEagle and RainbowHawk. *Heart Seeds: A Message from the Ancestors*. Minneapolis, MN: Beaver's Pond Press, 2004.

Liberating the Gatekeepers

Captured Light Industries. *What the Bleep Do We Know?* 2004. A Lord of the Wind Film. www.whatthebleep.com

Fritz, Robert. *The Path of Least Resistance: Learning to Become the Creative Force in Your Own Life*. New York: Fawcett Columbine, 1984.

Lipton, Bruce. *The Biology of Belief: Unleashing the Power of Consciousness, Matter, and Miracles*. Santa Rosa, CA: Mountain of Love/Elite Books, 2005.

Quinn, Daniel. *Ishmael*. New York: Bantam/Turner, 1992.

*Sams, Jamie. *Dancing the Dream: The Seven Sacred Paths of Human Transformation*. San Francisco: HarperCollins, 1999.

Conscious Dreamwork

*Harary, Keith, and Weintraub, Pamela. *Lucid Dreams in 30 Days: The Creative Sleep Program.* New York: St. Martin's Griffin, 1989.

*Moss, Robert. *Dreamgates: An Explorer's Guide to the Worlds of Soul, Imagination, and Life Beyond Death.* New York: Three Rivers Press, 1998.

*Sun Bear, Wabun Wind, and Shawnodese. *Dreaming with the Wheel: How to Interpret and Work with Your Dreams Using the Medicine Wheel.* New York: Fireside, 1994.

Journaling

*Cameron, Julia. *The Right to Write: An Invitation and Initiation into the Writing Life.* New York: Tarcher/Putnam, 1998.

*Baldwin, Christina. *Life's Companion: Journal Writing as a Spiritual Quest.* New York: Bantam Books, 1990.

*Baldwin, Christina. *Storycatcher: Making Sense of Our Lives through the Power and Practice of Story.* Novato, CA: New World Library, 2005.

*Grason, Sandy. *Journalution: Journaling to Awaken Your Inner Voice, Heal Your Life, and Manifest Your Dreams.* Novato, CA: New World Library, 2005.

Sacred Art

*Allen, Pat B. *Art Is a Spiritual Path: Engaging the Sacred through the Practice of Art and Writing.* Boston: Shambhala, 2005.

*Allen, Pat B. *Art Is a Way of Knowing.* Boston: Shambhala, 1995.

*Cornell, Judith. *Mandala: Luminous Symbols for Healing.* Wheaton, IL: Quest Books, 1994.

*Cornell, Judith. *The Mandala Healing Kit: Using Sacred Symbols for Spiritual and Emotional Healing.* Boulder, CO: Sounds True, 2005.

Collective Inquiry

*Baldwin, Christina. *Calling the Circle: The First and Future Culture*. Newberg, OR: SwanRaven, 1994.

*Brown, Juanita. *The World Café: Shaping our Futures through Conversations That Matter*. San Francisco: Berrett-Koehler, 2005.

*Garfield, Charles, Spring, Cindy, and Cahill, Sedonia. *Wisdom Circles: A Guide to Self-Discovery and Community Building in Small Groups*. New York: Hyperion, 1998.

*Isaacs, William. *Dialogue and the Art of Thinking Together: A Pioneering Approach to Communicating in Business and in Life*. New York: Currency, 1999.

ACKNOWLEDGMENTS

I am deeply grateful to each person that I have engaged with in the past twenty years about the spiritual journey of life. This has been a blessing and a very important part of my own soul evolution and the birth of this book. Their questions have guided me in exploring the Rainbow Wheel, and it is a blessing that they have included me in their soulwork process. Throughout the writing of this book I have been generously showered by the wondrous gifts of many. I greatly appreciate the guidance, wisdom, and grace of Pat Benson, my media consultant. Her enthusiasm and gentle nudging were invaluable, as were her insightful questions. Mary Byers, my skillful editor, has been a brilliant light, carefully shining the steps on the pathway of bringing this book to completion with much greater clarity. Thank you to the *i*Universe team for supporting me in successfully bringing this book to publication.

I have been able to write this book and do the work of the Rainbow Wheel because of the constant and immeasurable support of my husband, Wayne Feller. His open heart, gentleness, compassion, and love remind me every single day of what it means to be one's spiritual gift. He has breathed life into me and into the creation of this book. My son, Dan, has been calling me to be truly awake from the first moment of his life. I am blessed that he is here, and grateful for all that he has contributed to this book—his soulful questions, creative guidance, and artistic graphics. Wise elders—first and foremost my mother, father, grandmother Libby, and second mother (my husband's mother)—have nurtured and cared for me throughout my life. If not for them, I could not do this work.

My circle of family, friends, and healing companions is a gift of the highest order. These sisters and brothers of this amazing journey of life, along with all of their incredible children, are my constant teachers and my inspiration. They are each jewels, filled with indescribable beauty and light: Lynn, Susan, Ellen, Dennis, Seth, Cecelia, Helen, DancingEagle, BlackWolf, Chelsea, Ethan, Cary, Liam, Kayva, Melanie, Rose, Mary, Vivi, Roxane, Sharon, Barbra, Ellie, Catharine, Charlie, Jesse, Terese, Margurite, Joci, Jim, Jeremy, Angie, Phyllis, Shayna, Maya, Devi, Jackie, Jan, Nate, Kyle, Cathy, Steve, Sam, Sara, Jeanette, Mary Elizabeth, Asha, Rani, Debra, and so many, many other Beings. And the touch of my circle of healing guides has uplifted me—spiritually, emotionally, and (quite literally) physically—offering knowledge, understanding, and support, and giving me courage and hope.

I offer to all of you my love, admiration, and deep gratitude.

ABOUT THE AUTHOR

For twenty years, Jo Elise Friedman, Ph.D., has been drawing upon her work with the Rainbow Wheel, as well as her professional experience as an educator and group process facilitator, to nurture and engage people as they journey along their transformational pathways. Through spiritual mentoring she has provided support for consciously stepping through gateways to unfold life and evolve soul. While her work focuses on addressing the current questions arising for the individuals she mentors, Jo Elise has found that there is often a core underlying question attempting to surface: What is calling to be created in my life? She has found this many-layered question to be a powerful guiding force that fosters a sense of wonder and possibility as it draws one to a deeper place of exploration and soulwork.

Jo Elise is continually awed by what this search brings forth. The work of others inspires her to move forward with her own evolutionary work and the work of the Rainbow Wheel. In addition to her individual mentoring, Jo Elise has supported educational, government, nonprofit, and business organizations in creating their visions and strategic goals, while generating an expanded sense of spirit for their organization's collective work. Jo Elise lives in the St. Croix River Valley in Stillwater, Minnesota, with her husband and son. Visit her website at www.joelise.com.

978-0-595-43771-9
0-595-43771-0

LaVergne, TN USA
25 February 2010
174140LV00004B/4/A